Cambridge University Press

CAMBRIDGE
Primary Computing

Learner's Book 2

Jon Chippindall,
Ben Davies & Isabella Lieghio

CAMBRIDGE
UNIVERSITY PRESS

Shaftesbury Road, Cambridge CB2 8EA, United Kingdom

One Liberty Plaza, 20th Floor, New York, NY 10006, USA

477 Williamstown Road, Port Melbourne, VIC 3207, Australia

314–321, 3rd Floor, Plot 3, Splendor Forum, Jasola District Centre, New Delhi – 110025, India

103 Penang Road, #05–06/07, Visioncrest Commercial, Singapore 238467

Cambridge University Press & Assessment is part of the University of Cambridge.

We share the University's mission to contribute to society through the pursuit of education, learning and research at the highest international levels of excellence.

www.cambridge.org
Information on this title: www.cambridge.org/9781009309219

© Cambridge University Press & Assessment 2023

This publication is in copyright. Subject to statutory exception and to the provisions of relevant collective licensing agreements, no reproduction of any part may take place without the written permission of Cambridge University Press & Assessment.

20 19 18 17 16 15 14 13 12 11

Printed in Italy by L.E.G.O. S.p.A.

A catalogue record for this publication is available from the British Library

ISBN 978-1-009-30921-9 Paperback with Digital Access (1 Year)
ISBN 978-1-009-32042-9 Digital Learner's Book (1 Year)
ISBN 978-1-009-32041-2 eBook

Additional resources for this publication at www.cambridge.org/go

Cambridge University Press & Assessment has no responsibility for the persistence or accuracy of URLs for external or third-party internet websites referred to in this publication, and does not guarantee that any content on such websites is, or will remain, accurate or appropriate. Information regarding prices, travel timetables, and other factual information given in this work is correct at the time of first printing but Cambridge University Press & Assessment does not guarantee the accuracy of such information thereafter.

....

NOTICE TO TEACHERS IN THE UK
It is illegal to reproduce any part of this work in material form (including photocopying and electronic storage) except under the following circumstances:
(i) where you are abiding by a licence granted to your school or institution by the Copyright Licensing Agency;
(ii) where no such licence exists, or where you wish to exceed the terms of a licence, and you have gained the written permission of Cambridge University Press & Assessment;
(iii) where you are allowed to reproduce without permission under the provisions of Chapter 3 of the Copyright, Designs and Patents Act 1988, which covers, for example, the reproduction of short passages within certain types of educational anthology and reproduction for the purposes of setting examination questions.

....

Endorsement statement

Endorsement indicates that a resource has passed Cambridge International's rigorous quality-assurance process and is suitable to support the delivery of a Cambridge International curriculum framework. However, endorsed resources are not the only suitable materials available to support teaching and learning, and are not essential to be used to achieve the qualification. Resource lists found on the Cambridge International website will include this resource and other endorsed resources.

Any example answers to questions taken from past question papers, practice questions, accompanying marks and mark schemes included in this resource have been written by the authors and are for guidance only. They do not replicate examination papers. In examinations the way marks are awarded may be different. Any references to assessment and/or assessment preparation are the publisher's interpretation of the curriculum framework requirements. Examiners will not use endorsed resources as a source of material for any assessment set by Cambridge International.

While the publishers have made every attempt to ensure that advice on the qualification and its assessment is accurate, the official curriculum framework, specimen assessment materials and any associated assessment guidance materials produced by the awarding body are the only authoritative source of information and should always be referred to for definitive guidance. Cambridge International recommends that teachers consider using a range of teaching and learning resources based on their own professional judgement of their students' needs.

Cambridge International has not paid for the production of this resource, nor does Cambridge International receive any royalties from its sale. For more information about the endorsement process, please visit www.cambridgeinternational.org/endorsed-resources

Cambridge International copyright material in this publication is reproduced under licence and remains the intellectual property of Cambridge Assessment International Education.

Third party websites and resources referred to in this publication have not been endorsed by Cambridge Assessment International Education.

Introduction

Welcome to Stage 2 of Cambridge Primary Computing!

Computers play an important part in our lives.

We use them to do lots of things.

This book will help you explore some of the different ways that we can use computers.

There are lots of interesting topics in this book.

They will help you to understand:

- how you can collect data to answer questions
- why algorithms need to be precise
- why repeat commands are used in programs
- the types of jobs that computers do better than humans
- the types of information that can be shared through networks.

This book also contains lots of activities.

These are designed to be completed with your classmates.

This will allow you to discuss what you have learnt.

These activities will help you learn how to do things with technology.

The activities are things like writing computer programs to create animations and making block graphs and pictograms from data.

We hope this book makes you want to learn more about the ways computers are used.

It may give you some ideas about how computers will be used in the future.

Jon Chippindall, Ben Davies and Isabella Lieghio

Contents

How to use this book   6

1 Computational thinking and programming

1.1 Precise algorithms   9
1.2 Debugging programs   25
1.3 Animal animations   42
1.4 Repeat, repeat, repeat   61

2 Managing data

2.1 Data all around   78
2.2 Problem solvers   91
2.3 Presenting data   101

3 Networks and digital communication

3.1 Connect to a network   115
3.2 Why have a network?   129

4 Computer systems

4.1 Hardware and software   143
4.2 Different types of computer   161
4.3 Computers, humans and robots   178

Glossary   197
Acknowledgements   205

> Note for teachers: Throughout the resource there is a symbol to indicate where additional digital only content is provided. This content can be accessed through the Digital Learner's Book on Cambridge GO. It can be launched either from the Media tab or directly from the page. The symbol that denotes additional digital content is: 🔗. The source files can also be downloaded from the Source files tab on Cambridge GO. In addition, this tab contains a teacher guidance document which supports the delivery of digital activities and programing tasks in this Learner's Book.

How to use this book

How to use this book

In this book you will find lots of different features to help your learning.

What you will learn in the topic.

> **We are going to:**
> - learn how to debug a program
> - find out why it is helpful to split a program into smaller steps
> - predict the outcome of an algorithm

Important words to learn.

> block graph   pictogram
> form   present
> graph

A reminder about what you already know and an activity to start you off.

> **Getting started**
> **What do you already know?**
> - An algorithm is a precise set of instructions.
> - You have made algorithms into programs using Bee-Bots.
> - You have debugged algorithms and programs.

Fun activities about computing. Sometimes, you will use a computer.

> **Activity 3**
> **Minecraft towers**
> You will need:
> a desktop computer or laptop with a keyboard and internet access, a pencil and paper or a whiteboard pen and mini whiteboard, website link from your teacher or the Digital Learner's Book
>
> You will use Minecraft for this activity. Your teacher will show you how to use the tools.

Some activities don't need a computer. These are called unplugged activities. They help you to understand important ideas about computing.

> **Unplugged activity 1**
> **Get out of the maze**
> You will need:
> a pencil and paper, or a whiteboard pen and mini whiteboard
>
> You will work in small groups. Your teacher is going to make a maze for each group. This can be in the school hall or on the playground.
> Look at the maze. Can you work out how to get through it?
> In your groups, write an algorithm for directions to get through the maze. You can write your algorithm in words or draw arrows.

Sometimes, you will see this question. It will help you to think about your work.

> **How are we doing?**
> Check with your partner. Did you spot the bug in their algorithm?

How to use this book

Tasks to help you to practise what you have learnt.

Programming tasks are in Unit 1. ⟶

> **Programming task 2**
>
> **ScratchJr challenges**
>
> You will need:
> a computer or tablet running ScratchJr
>
> Look at your program from Programming task 1 in ScratchJr. Complete these steps for each of the following challenges:
> 1 Make the change.

Practical tasks are in Unit 2. ⟶

> **Practical task 1**
>
> **Collect your own data**
>
> You will need:
> a desktop computer, laptop or tablet with internet access, source file **2.4_collecting_data**
>
> Think about something you would like to find out from your classmates. Here are some things you could ask them about:
> - number of siblings (brothers and sisters)
> - what pets they have

Look out for this icon. You are going to do an activity at the computer using a source file or website link. This content can be found in the Digital Learner's Book on Cambridge GO. Your teacher will help you to get started. ⟶

Questions that help you to check that you understand the topic. Are you ready to move on? ⟶

> **Questions**
> 1 Can you point to the repeat command?
> 2 What do you think the number 4 means?

Things to remember when you are using a computer. ⟶

> **Stay safe!**
>
> Arun is careful not to share personal details online, like his address, without his parents' permission.

Interesting facts connected to the topic. ⟶

> **Did you know?**
>
> Some computer programmers work in pairs to make programs. We call this pair programming. It helps them find bugs in their programs.

How to use this book

Questions to help you think about how you learn.

> Why do you think it is sometimes easier to find bugs in someone else's algorithm?

What you have learnt in the topic.

Look what I can do!
- ☐ I know how to debug a program.
- ☐ I can split a problem into steps.
- ☐ I know I should keep testing my programs to help find bugs.
- ☐ I know why working with others can help me to debug.

At the end of each unit, there is a project for you to carry out, using what you have learnt. You might make something or solve a problem.

Project

Make your own animation program in ScratchJr

You will need:
source file **1.3_planning_grid**, pens and pencils, a computer or tablet running ScratchJr

In this project, you will make your own ScratchJr animation. You will work in pairs.

Your animation should:
- have two sprites
- use commands in the 'Look' and 'Motion' command groups
- use repeat commands.

Questions that cover what you have learnt in the unit. If you can answer these, you are ready to move on to the next unit.

Check your progress

1. Why do we use passwords?
2. Which of these questions would have an answer in numbers?
   A What is your favourite book?
   B What is your shoe size?
   C Do you like watching cartoons?
3. Describe the difference between a statistical question and a non-statistical question.
4. Which sort of question could you solve by collecting data? Statistical or non-statistical?
5. This is one of the questions on Zara's form: 'What is your favourite subject at school?'
   What choices would you give people for this question?

1 Computational thinking and programming

> 1.1 Precise algorithms

We are going to:
- understand why algorithms need to be clear and correct
- write our own algorithms
- find and fix errors in algorithms.

algorithm   error
bug   instructions
debug   precise
directions   test

Getting started

What do you already know?
- An algorithm is a set of instructions.
- The instructions must be in the correct sequence (order).
- Things which are wrong in algorithms (errors) are called bugs.

1 Computational thinking and programming

> **Continued**
>
> **Now try this!**
>
> Zara has written an algorithm for arriving at school.
>
> 1. Go into the cloakroom.
> 2. Take off your backpack.
> 3. Take off your coat.
> 4. Put your coat on your hook.
> 5. Put your backpack on the hook.
>
> Work with a partner.
>
> Write or draw an algorithm for a school activity.
>
> You can write an algorithm for getting ready for a sports lesson or going to lunch.
>
> Remember to put each instruction in a different step. A step is one part of an instruction.
>
> Now act out your algorithm for another pair. Ask them to check if it is correct.
>
> Did you miss a step out or put some steps in the wrong order?

1.1 Precise algorithms

Directions as algorithms

When you tell someone how to get to a place, you are giving them **directions**.

Directions are a type of **algorithm**. We already know that algorithms are a set of instructions. Here is an example.

Arun is having a birthday party. He made an invitation and included some directions, or an algorithm, to find his house.

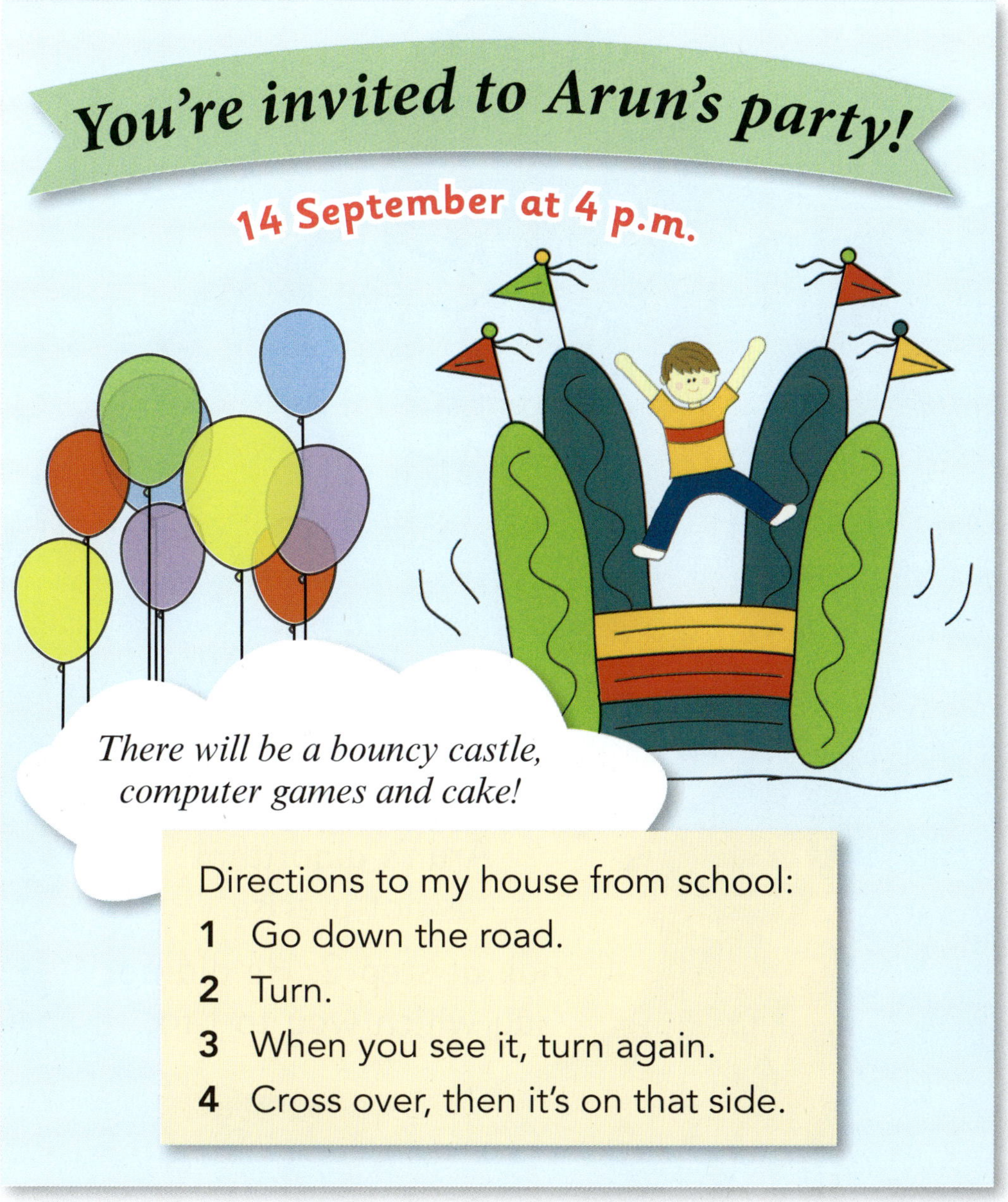

You're invited to Arun's party!

14 September at 4 p.m.

There will be a bouncy castle, computer games and cake!

Directions to my house from school:
1. Go down the road.
2. Turn.
3. When you see it, turn again.
4. Cross over, then it's on that side.

11

1 Computational thinking and programming

Questions

1. Is Arun's algorithm helpful? Why or why not?
2. Do you think his friends will find his house?

It is important that algorithms are **precise**.

When an algorithm is precise, it includes all the information that people need to follow it.

> **Stay safe!**
>
> Arun is careful not to share personal details, like his address, online without asking his parents first.

Arun's algorithm is not precise.
Look at step 2. He did not say which way to turn.

1.1 Precise algorithms

Arun has changed his invitation.

What has he done to make his invitation more precise?
Look back at his first invitation to remind yourself.

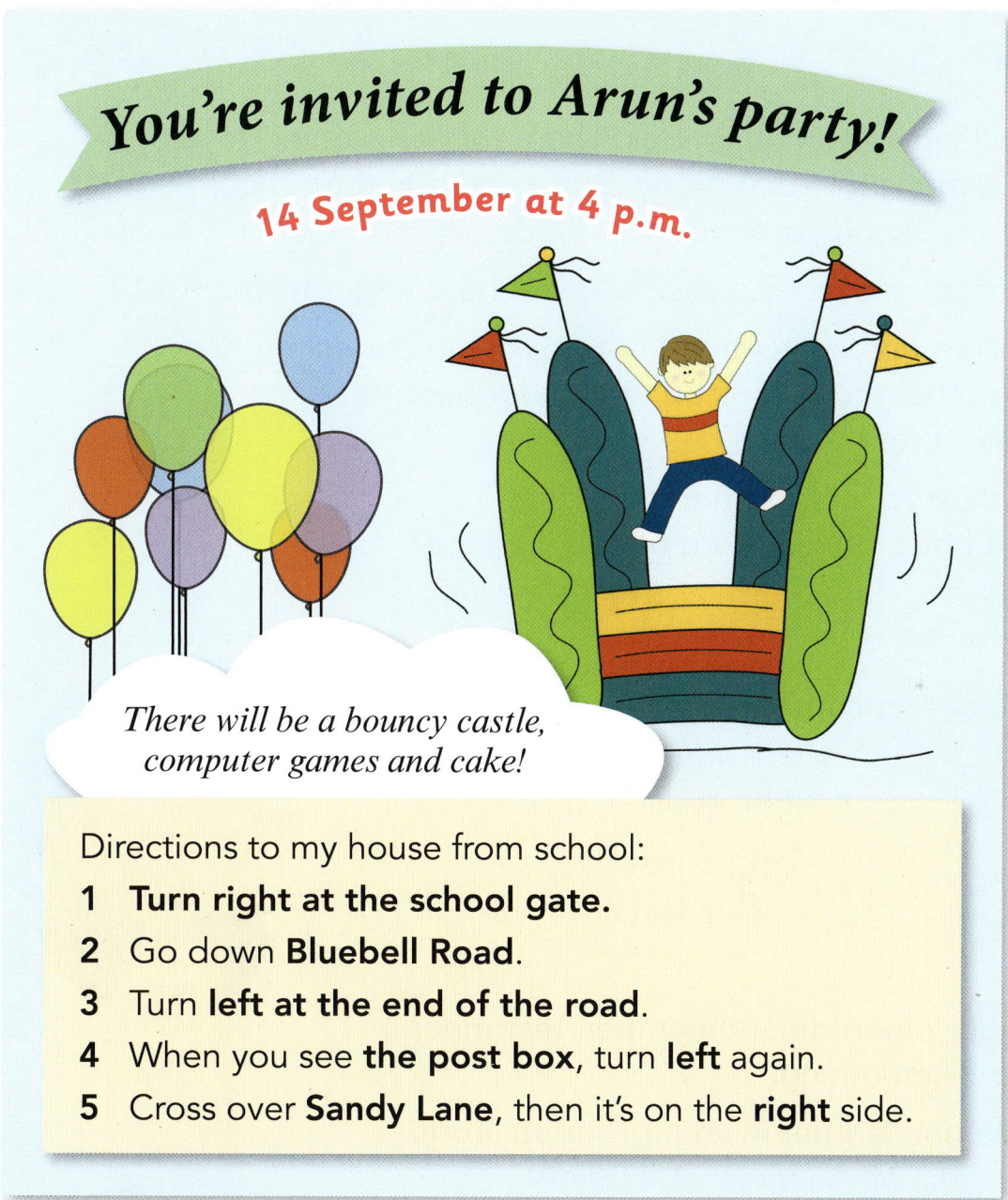

In this topic, we are going to practise writing precise algorithms.

1 Computational thinking and programming

Unplugged activity 1

Get out of the maze

> **You will need:**
> a pencil and paper, or a whiteboard pen and mini whiteboard

You will work in small groups. Your teacher is going to make a maze for each group. This can be in the school hall or on the playground.

Look at the maze. Can you work out how to get through it?

In your groups, write an algorithm for directions to get through the maze. You can write your algorithm in words or draw arrows.

Make sure your algorithm is precise!
Does it have all the information you need?

To turn a corner, you need to put in a left quarter turn or a right quarter turn.

This is just like Bee-Bots!

Test your algorithm. Remember, test means to check something.

Choose one learner in your group to stand at the start of the maze and follow the algorithm to test it.

14

1.1 Precise algorithms

Continued

How are we doing?

Was your algorithm precise? Check if your algorithm had this information:

- where to start
- how many steps to take in each direction
- which way to turn (left or right) at each corner
- how far to turn (quarter turns).

Draw a star for each point that you included in your algorithm.

1 Computational thinking and programming

Unplugged activity 2

Dance move algorithms

> **You will need:**
> a pencil and paper, or a whiteboard pen and mini whiteboard

You are going to write an algorithm for a dance.

When your partner follows the algorithm, their dance should match yours.

Part A: Make your algorithm

1. Think of a simple dance. It can be three or four moves such as hand waves, turns or jumps.
2. Practise your dance.
3. Now write an algorithm for your dance.

Make sure your algorithm is precise, so others can easily follow it. What information do you need to give?

Remember, when an algorithm is precise, it includes all the information needed to follow it.

16

1.1 Precise algorithms

> **Continued**
>
> Now you are going to check your algorithm.
>
> **Part B: Test your algorithm**
>
> 1. Make a group with two other learners.
>   One of the learners will follow your algorithm.
>
>   You will perform your dance at the same time.
>
>   The other learner will check whether both of your dances match. If your algorithm was precise, they should be exactly the same!
>
> 2. Discuss whether your dances were the same or different.
>
> 3. If they were different, change your algorithm. Include more information to make it more precise.
>
>   Then make a new group with two different learners.
>
>   Ask someone else to follow it while the other person checks it. Is your algorithm more precise now?

Watch someone follow your algorithm. It can help you to see where your algorithm isn't precise. Why do you think it helps?

1 Computational thinking and programming

Splitting tasks into smaller steps

Splitting tasks into smaller parts, or steps, can be useful. It means we can look at one step of the task at a time.

We can also split algorithms into smaller steps. This can help us to make more precise algorithms.

When we have written a precise algorithm for one step, we can then write the next one.

Marcus wants to make a sandwich, but he does not know where to start.

Sofia explains that he needs to split the task into smaller steps.

1. Get two pieces of bread.
2. Spread some butter on them.
3. Add slices of cheese to one piece of bread.
4. Put the other piece of bread on top.
5. Ask an adult to cut the sandwich in half.

In the next activity, we will split a task into smaller steps. We will write the algorithm for one step at a time.

1.1 Precise algorithms

Activity 3

Minecraft towers

> **You will need:**
> a desktop computer or laptop with a keyboard and internet access,
> a pencil and paper or a whiteboard pen and mini whiteboard,
> the website link from your teacher or the Digital Learner's Book

You will use Minecraft for this activity. Your teacher will show you how to use the tools.

Part A: Build a tower

Work with a partner.

Look at the picture. Build a tower like this in Minecraft using different blocks. You can choose which colours you would like to use.

Your tower can be up to two blocks tall and four blocks wide.

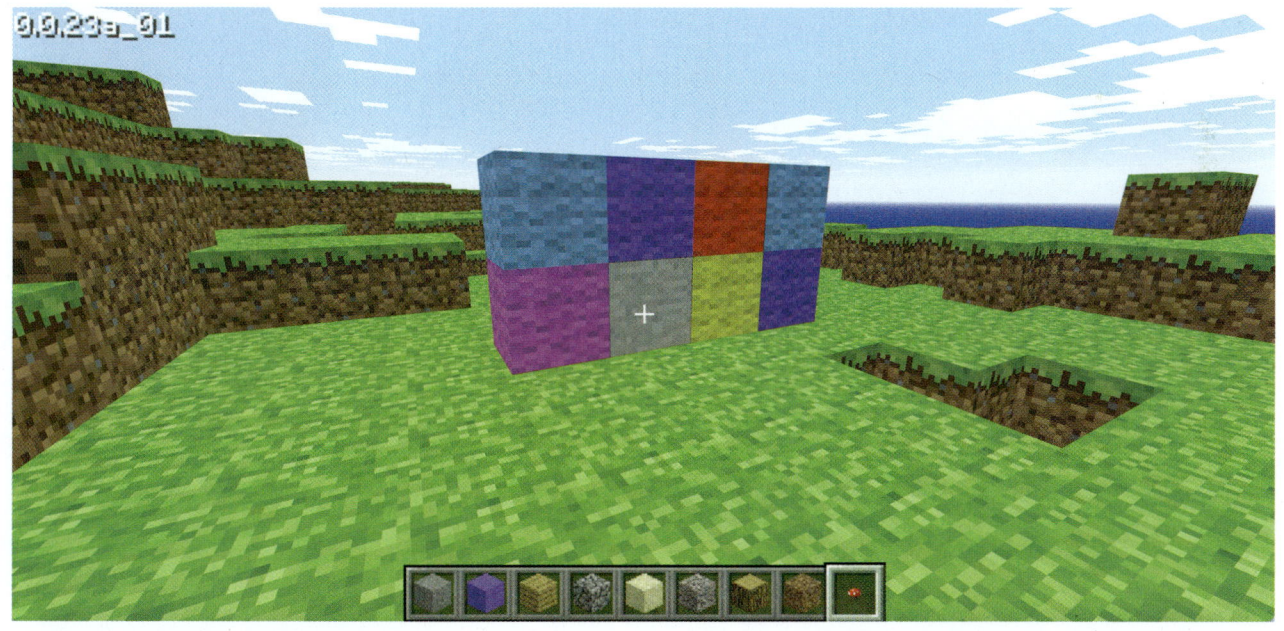

1 Computational thinking and programming

Continued

Part B: Write an algorithm

You are going to write a precise algorithm so that someone else can build your tower.

Split the task into smaller steps. Write the algorithm for one row of blocks at a time.

Here are the first two steps of the algorithm to make the tower in the picture:

Continue the steps to complete the algorithm.

> 1. Place a bright pink block.
> 2. Place a grey block to the right of the pink block. The two blocks must touch.

Remember to include:
- the colour of each block
- exactly where to put it.

How are we doing?

Work with another pair. Let them build your tower using your algorithm.

Does their tower look the same as yours? If not, change your algorithm to make it more precise.

The other pair can try it again.

1.1 Precise algorithms

Did you know?

Large things like bridges have to be built one step at a time.

A team of people work together to split the task into smaller steps.

It is important that each step is correct otherwise the bridge may not be safe.

You split tasks into smaller parts in your schoolwork.

When you write a story, you can split it into a start, middle and end.

Can you think of any other examples where you split a task into parts? Why does it help?

1 Computational thinking and programming

Debugging algorithms

Even when we take lots of care to write precise algorithms, they can still have mistakes in them.

These mistakes are called **errors**. We already know that errors in algorithms are called **bugs**.

Let's think about how we can look for and correct bugs in our algorithms. This is called **debugging**.

In the next topic we will move on to debugging programs.

Zara has written an algorithm for getting dressed.

Can you find the bug in Zara's algorithm?

1. Put on your trousers.
2. Put on your T-shirt.
3. Put on your shoes.
4. Put on your socks.

1.1 Precise algorithms

Two of the most common bugs in algorithms are:

- forgetting to include **instructions** (a set of words or pictures that tell you what to do or how to make something work)
- putting instructions in the wrong order.

Try not to make these mistakes!

Now you are going to play a game. It will help you and your partner learn how to spot bugs.

Unplugged activity 4

Can you find my bug?

You will need:
a pencil and paper or a whiteboard pen and mini whiteboard

You are going to hide a bug in an algorithm.
Your partner has to find it.

1 Computational thinking and programming

Continued

Write an algorithm for an everyday task, such as getting dressed or making breakfast.

Include one bug. You can leave out a step, or put steps in the wrong order.

Look at your partner's algorithm. Can you debug their algorithm? Tell your partner what the bug is.

Find another partner. Try to debug your new partner's algorithm.

How many algorithms can you debug?

There is a bug in my algorithm. I did not get a bowl before pouring the cereal!

Look what I can do!

☐ I can explain why algorithms need to be precise.

☐ I can write a precise algorithm.

☐ I can find and fix errors in algorithms.

1.2 Debugging programs

We are going to:
- learn how to debug a program
- find out why it is helpful to split a program into smaller steps
- predict the outcome of an algorithm
- understand why we need to keep testing our program
- understand why it is helpful to work together to debug programs.

algorithm   predict
bug   programs
command   run
debug   test

Getting started

What do you already know?
- You have written algorithms for everyday tasks.
- You have debugged everyday algorithms.
- You have turned algorithms into programs on a Bee-Bot.
- You have spotted bugs in Bee-Bot programs.

1 Computational thinking and programming

> **Continued**
>
> **Now try this!**
>
> You may have used Bee-Bots before.
>
> You might have turned algorithms into programs. Programs are instructions that make a computer do a task.
>
> You might have used the commands (instructions) on the Bee-Bot to make programs.
>
> Three of the commands on this Bee-Bot are hidden.
>
> Discuss with a partner.
> Which commands are missing?
> What do the missing commands do?

Bee-Bot town

In this topic, you are going to move a Bee-Bot around a town grid.

1.2 Debugging programs

You are also going to write an algorithm (a set of instructions) for the Bee-Bot. You can do this using arrows.

Did you remember what the commands do?
The Bee-Bot's four movement command buttons make it:

- move forward one Bee-Bot step

- move backward one Bee-Bot step

- turn a quarter turn right

- turn a quarter turn left.

To run the Bee-Bot, press GO.

This means the Bee-Bot will follow the instructions that you gave it.

To clear the program stored in the Bee-Bot press X.

Unplugged activity 1

Let's explore the town

Have a look at the Bee-Bot town on the next page.

Marcus has written an algorithm for a Bee-Bot so it can visit one of the places in the town.

The Bee-Bot will start on the start square and face in the direction shown by the arrow.

1 Computational thinking and programming

Continued

This is the algorithm Marcus has written:

Where do you **predict** the Bee-Bot will finish? Discuss it with a partner.

Remember, predict means say what you think will happen.

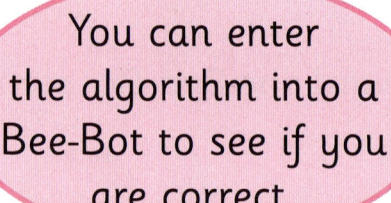

1.2 Debugging programs

Now it is time to try some challenges from Zara!

Programming task 1

Bee-Bot challenges

You will need:
a Bee-Bot, a Bee-Bot town grid made from source file **1.1_town_grid**, a pencil and paper or a whiteboard pen and mini whiteboard

For each challenge:

1 Write the algorithm. You can use arrows for this.
2 Enter your algorithm as a program on the Bee-Bot.
3 Run the program to see whether you are correct.

Remember to clear old programs stored in the Bee-Bot by pressing the 'X'.

Can you get the Bee-Bot to finish in the following places?

1 At the playground.

Here are the first three commands to help you:

2 At the swimming pool.

29

1 Computational thinking and programming

> **Continued**
>
> **3** At the school. It must go through the sports field.

"Your Bee-Bot might not go the same way as others. That's OK, as long as it still goes to the right places."

Debugging

When challenges get harder, it is easy to make mistakes.

We know that errors in algorithms or programs are called bugs. When we find and fix bugs, it is called debugging.

Arun has a top tip for how to find bugs in Bee-Bot programs.

Test your algorithm before programming your Bee-Bot. Remember, test means to check something.

One way you can test your algorithm is by moving a paper Bee-Bot through each step of an algorithm.

This is how you can spot any bugs before programming it. Once you have found the bugs, you can fix them.

We will learn how to improve our debugging skills in this topic.

1 Computational thinking and programming

Unplugged activity 2

Paper Bee-Bots

You will need:
source file **1.2_paper_beebot**, the Bee-Bot town grid, colouring pencils, scissors, a pencil and paper or a whiteboard pen and mini whiteboard

Colour in your Bee-Bot, then cut it out.

Place your Bee-Bot on the start square. Make sure it is pointing the right way.

Arun has written some algorithms to get the Bee-Bot to different places.

Check Arun's algorithms. Are they correct or can you see a bug? Correct any bugs you find.

Move your paper Bee-Bot on the town grid to follow the steps.

Remember, each new algorithm begins at the start square.

1

2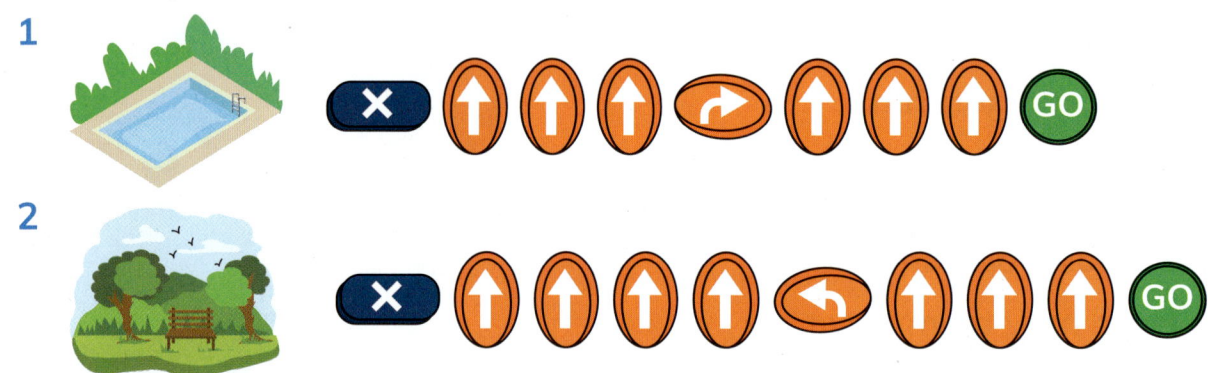

How are we doing?

Tell a partner about the bugs you found in Arun's algorithms.

What changes would you make to debug Arun's algorithms?

1.2 Debugging programs

Zara also has a top tip for debugging.

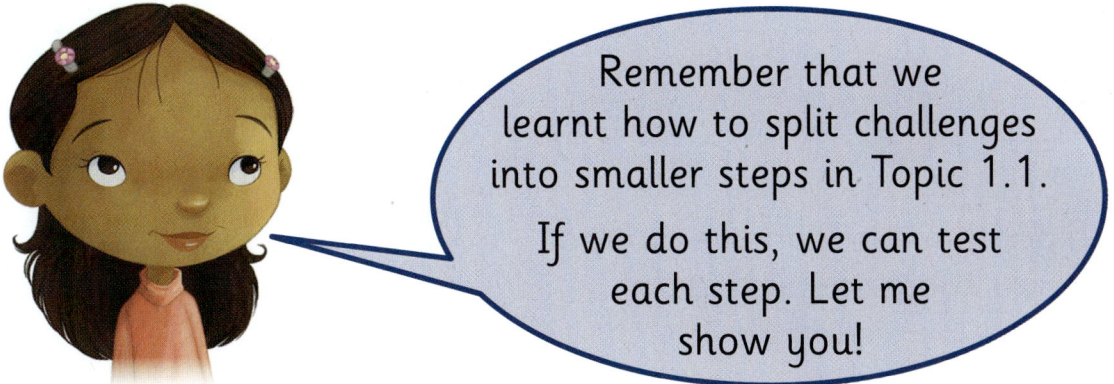

Remember that we learnt how to split challenges into smaller steps in Topic 1.1. If we do this, we can test each step. Let me show you!

Zara has been given a challenge:

Using the same town grid, get the Bee-Bot to the shop. It will start on the start square and needs to pass through the sports field on its way.

To make this challenge easier, Zara splits it into two steps.

1 Computational thinking and programming

Step 1: First, she writes the algorithm to get from the start to the sports field.

Zara tests her algorithm. She can use a paper Bee-Bot. She checks there are no bugs.

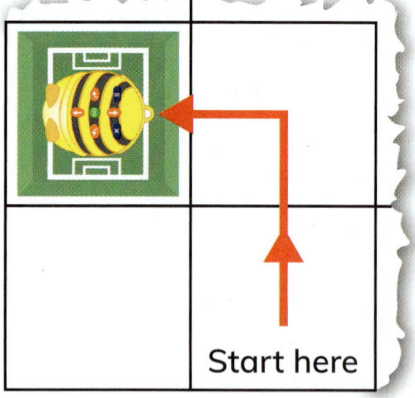

Step 2: Next, Zara writes an algorithm to get from the sports field to the shop.

Zara has to think about which way the Bee-Bot is facing.

Zara doesn't use the 'X' as she doesn't want to clear the first part of her program.

   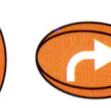  

Zara tests her algorithm regularly.

This means she keeps testing it each time she adds one or two commands.

She does this by using a paper Bee-Bot to act out the commands.

Testing her algorithm like this helps Zara to spot bugs straight away. This makes it easier to fix them.

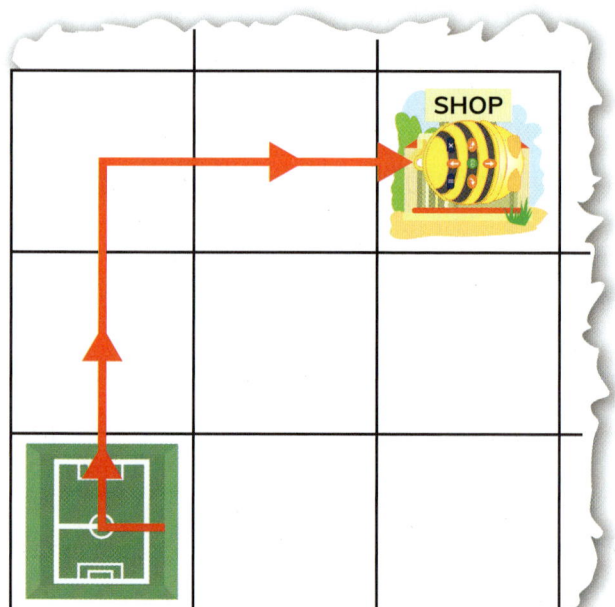

1.2 Debugging programs

Unplugged activity 3

Check Zara's algorithm

> You will need:
> your paper Bee-Bot, the Bee-Bot town grid

Zara now has the whole algorithm for the challenge.

Can you check it for her too? Use your paper Bee-Bot and town grid.

Remember, she is trying to get the Bee-Bot to the shop but wants it to pass through the sports field on the way.

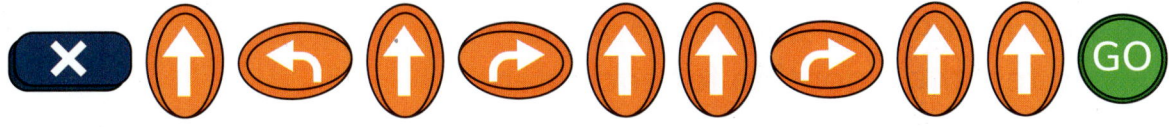

Instructions to get to sports field | Instructions to get from sports field to shop

Did you know?

This is Grace Hopper. She was one of the first programmers to use the word 'debug'.

1 Computational thinking and programming

Programming task 2

One step at a time

> You will need:
> a Bee-Bot, the Bee-Bot town grid, a paper Bee-Bot (optional),
> a pencil and paper or a whiteboard pen and mini whiteboard

Use Zara's debugging top tip to try these challenges using your town grid. Remember, Zara's top tip is to split each challenge into smaller steps.

Follow the instructions below for each challenge.

1. Split the challenge into smaller steps. Write and test the algorithm for each step before adding more instructions.

2. Regularly test your algorithm to check that there are no bugs. You can use your paper Bee-Bot.

3. Program your algorithm into the Bee-Bot when you are happy that it is correct. Run the program. Is it correct?

Continued

Challenge 1: Can you get the Bee-Bot to finish at the swimming pool but pass over the playground?

Challenge 2: Can you get the Bee-Bot to finish at the school but pass over the shop?

Challenge 3: Can you get the Bee-Bot to finish at the shop but pass over the sports field first and then the school?

Number 3 is hard! Do not worry if you cannot finish it.

How am I doing?

Copy this table into your notebook to keep track of how you are doing.

Challenge	Did you write a program? (✓ / ✗)	Did you have any bugs in your program? (✓ / ✗)	Did you fix the bugs? (✓ / ✗)	Did you finish the challenge? (✓ / ✗)
1				
2				
3				

Show a partner your table and look at their table.
Which challenges did they complete? What did they find difficult?

1 Computational thinking and programming

Working together

Working together can help us to debug algorithms or programs because we can talk through them with our partner.

Saying the steps aloud often helps us to spot bugs.

It is also often easier to debug something you have not written yourself.

> Why do you think it is sometimes easier to find bugs in someone else's algorithm?

Did you know?

Some programmers put a rubber duck on the top of their computer. They talk through their programs with it to help them spot bugs!

1.2 Debugging programs

Programming task 3

Debugging together

You will need:
a Bee-Bot, the Bee-Bot town grid, a paper Bee-Bot (optional), a pencil and paper or a whiteboard pen and mini whiteboard

Use your town grid. Add six trees to the squares shown below.

1 Computational thinking and programming

Continued

In this activity, your Bee-Bot cannot pass over a square with a tree in it.

1 First, write an algorithm for each challenge.

   Then read this aloud to your partner.
   This will help you to spot any bugs.

   Your partner can also use a paper Bee-Bot to help you test your algorithm.

2 Next, program the Bee-Bot.

Challenge 1: Can you get the Bee-Bot to finish at the swimming pool but pass over the sports field?

Challenge 2: Can you get the Bee-Bot to finish at the park but pass over the swimming pool?

Some people say that you can spend the same amount of time debugging programs as you spent writing them.

Do not worry if your program has bugs in it! That's normal.

1.2 Debugging programs

How do you find and correct errors in other subjects? Do you use any of the ideas we have looked at in this topic, like splitting a problem into smaller steps or working with someone else?

If you don't use these methods, can you use them? Discuss with a partner.

Look what I can do!

- [ ] I know how to debug a program.
- [ ] I can split a problem into steps.
- [ ] I know I should keep testing my programs to help find bugs.
- [ ] I know why working with others can help me to debug.

1 Computational thinking and programming

> 1.3 Animal animations

We are going to:

- follow an algorithm for a simple animation
- understand that programs tell computers how to run algorithms
- learn how to turn an algorithm into a program in ScratchJr.

algorithm programming language
animation ScratchJr
code sprite
command trigger
motion
program

Getting started

What do you already know?

- An algorithm is a precise set of instructions.
- You have turned algorithms into programs using Bee-Bots.
- You have debugged algorithms and programs.

1.3 Animal animations

Continued

Now try this!

Sofia wants her Bee-Bot to move in a square. Here is the algorithm she has written:

Can you test the algorithm for Sofia?
Discuss with a partner:

- Is there a bug in Sofia's algorithm?
- How would you fix the bug?
- Does it matter where the Bee-Bot starts?

Can you use any of the skills you learnt in Topic 1.2?

1 Computational thinking and programming

An animation for ScratchJr

You have turned an algorithm into a program using a Bee-Bot.

In this topic, we will turn an algorithm into a program using a computer.

Here is an algorithm for a simple **animation** (a moving image created by a computer) about a snake and a frog.

1.3 Animal animations

The algorithm includes information about how the characters move and what they say.

Work with a partner. Act out the animation by following the algorithm. Take turns to be each animal.

We will get a computer to follow this algorithm.

We can tell a computer how to follow an algorithm by creating a program.

A program is instructions that are in a language the computer understands.

This is called a **programming language**. **ScratchJr** is a programming language.

> Do you remember programming Bee-Bots?
>
> You pressed buttons to give the Bee-Bot instructions it understood.

Programs are made using single commands. Each command gives the computer an instruction to do something.

Lots of commands together can be called **code**.

Did you know?

There are hundreds of different programming languages. Don't worry! We will just be learning ScratchJr in this topic.

1   Computational thinking and programming

Marcus's ScratchJr program

Marcus wants to create a program in ScratchJr.
He wants a rocket to blast upwards from the moon.

The object or character our program controls is called a **sprite**.
Marcus has added a rocket sprite and a moon background.

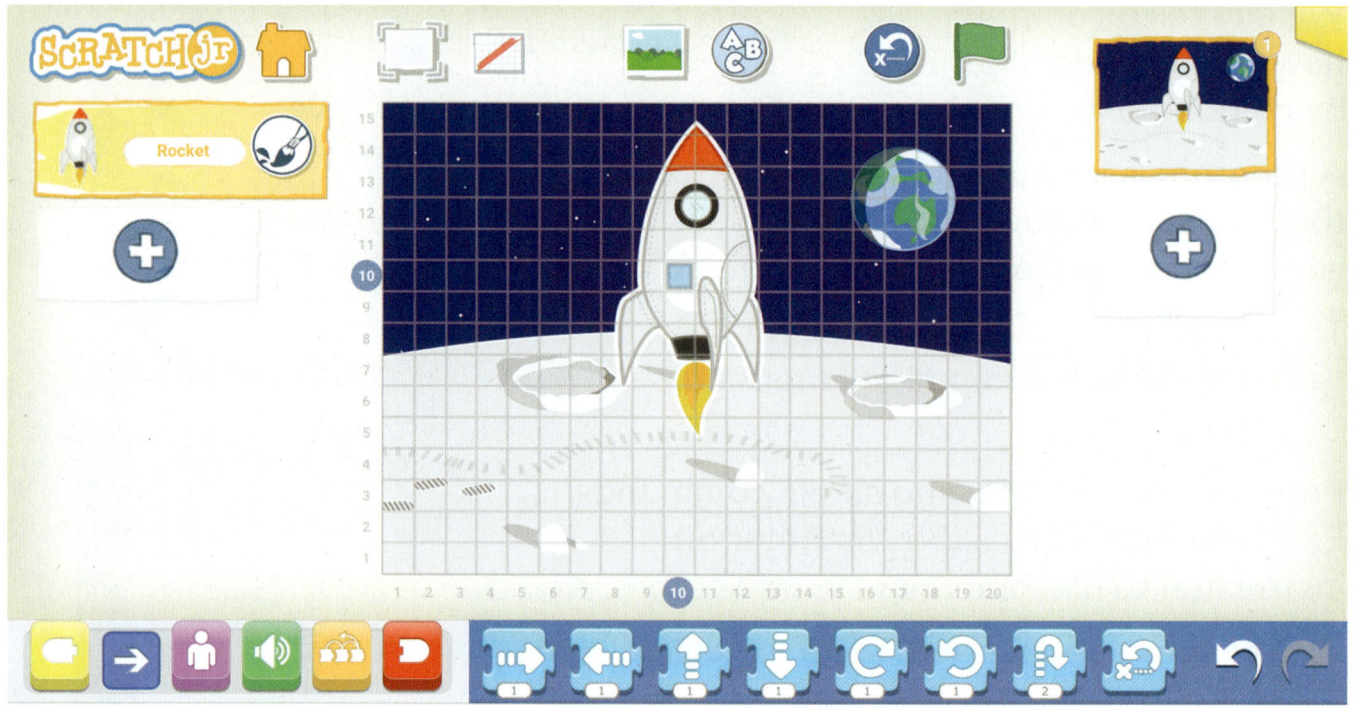

Marcus will now add commands to create a program.

Commands in ScratchJr are grouped together in the menu according to what they do.

You can choose a command by tapping on one of the groups in the commands menu. The menu looks like this:

Can you spot it in the picture above?

46

1.3 Animal animations

The commands have small pictures on them to help explain what they do. All the commands in a group are the same colour.

The table shows some of the groups of commands in the menu. You will learn about some of the other commands in Topic 1.4.

Command group	Single commands
Trigger commands	Trigger means to make something start. Trigger commands start programs.
Motion commands	Motion means to move. Motion commands make the sprites move. This is like the commands on the Bee-Bot that make it move.
Look commands	These change how the sprites look or gets them to say things.

Marcus has created a program for his rocket using three commands.

I made the program by dragging commands into the white part at the bottom of ScratchJr.
I put the commands together like jigsaw pieces.

1 Computational thinking and programming

Marcus followed these steps to make his program:

1. First, he tapped on the yellow 'Trigger commands' group.
2. Then he dragged a single yellow 'Trigger command' into the white part.
3. Next, he tapped on the blue 'Motion commands' group.
4. Then he dragged two blue 'Motion commands' into the white part.

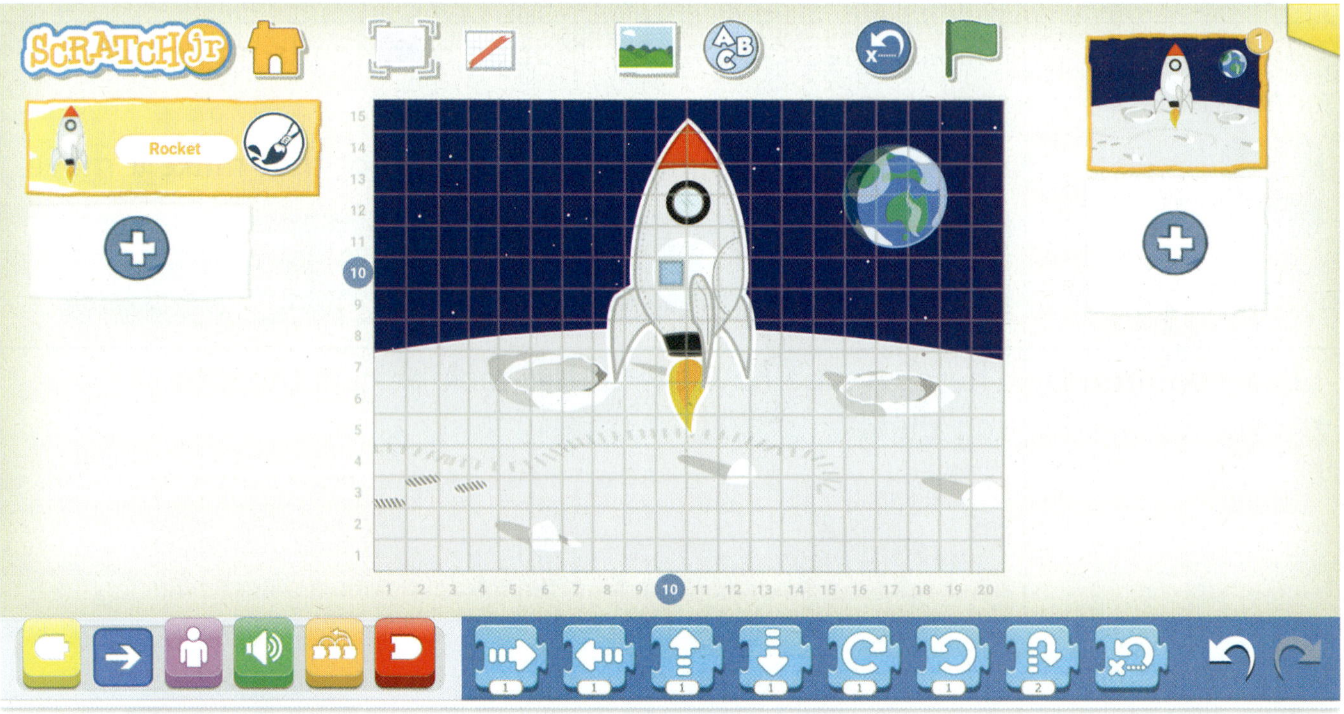

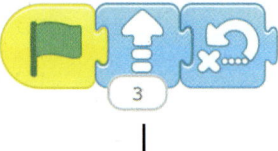

This is Marcus's program.

48

Let's look at the commands in Marcus's program.

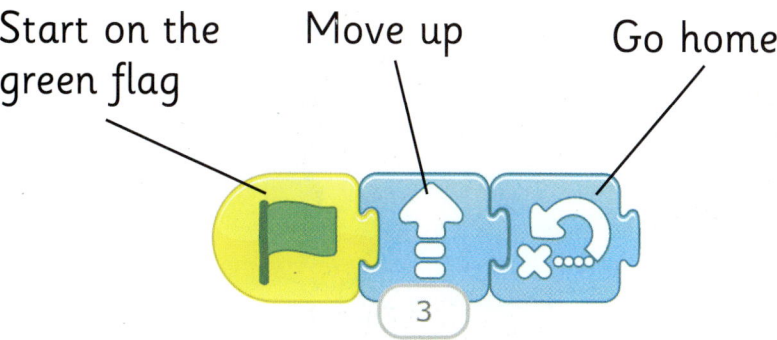

Start on the green flag

Move up

Go home

- Marcus has started his program with a trigger command: 'Start on green flag'.

  This means Marcus's program will run when the green flag at the top of the screen is tapped.

- When Marcus runs the program, the 'Move up' command will make the rocket sprite move up the screen.

  There is a small box with a number beneath the command. This tells the sprite how many grid squares to move up.

  (You may not be able to see the grid squares, but remember the Bee-Bot's grid squares. It is like that grid.)

- Next, the 'Go home' command will make the rocket go back to where it started.

Question

1 Discuss with a partner. Can you explain what Marcus's program will do when it is run?

1 Computational thinking and programming

Programming task 1

Exploring ScratchJr

> You will need:
> a computer or tablet running ScratchJr

Work with a partner. Open a new ScratchJr project by tapping the '+' button on the home screen.

When a new ScratchJr project is opened, the sprite (character) is always a cat. We will look at how to change this later.

Add the 'Start on green flag' trigger command by dragging it to the white part at the bottom of the screen.

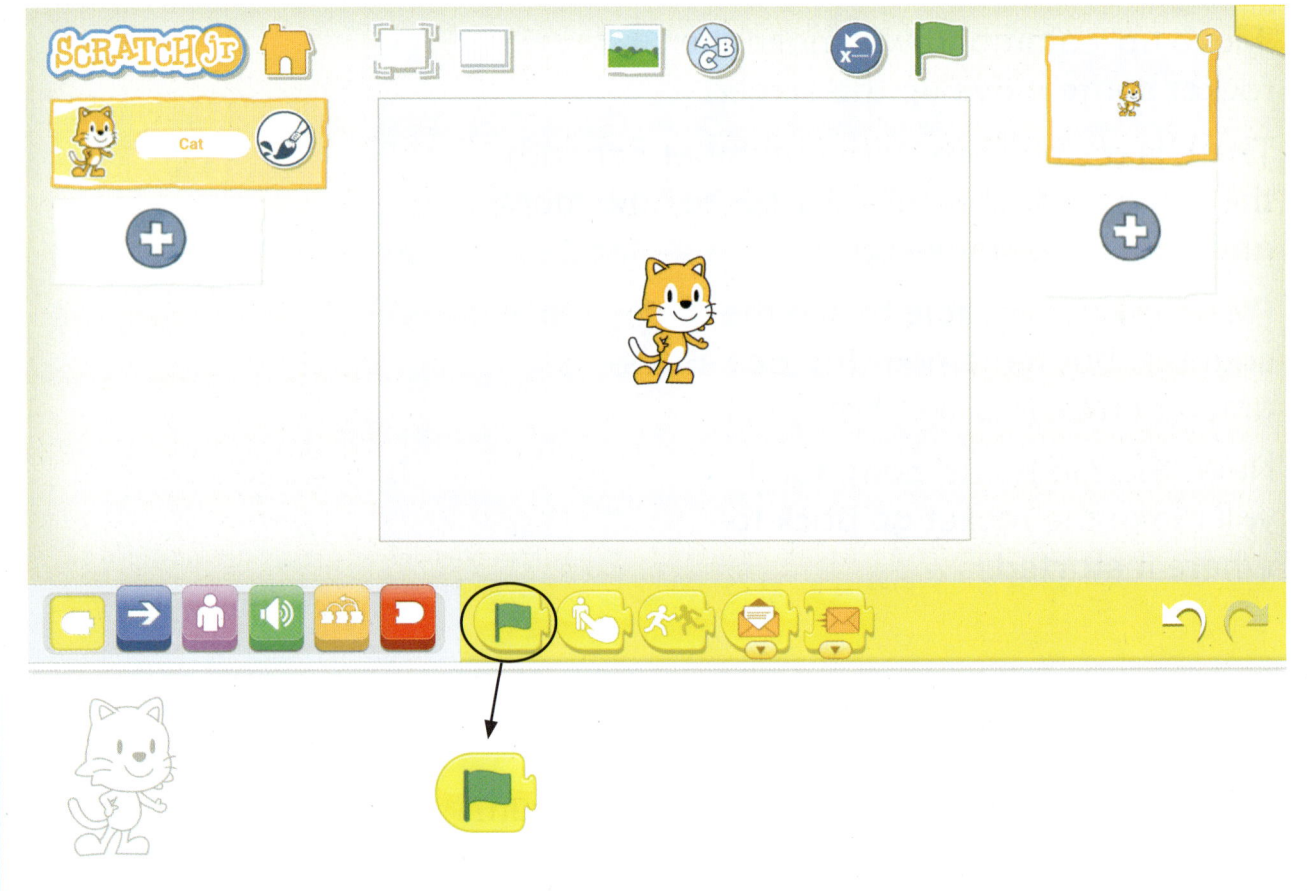

1.3 Animal animations

Continued

Look at some of the different commands in the 'Motion' and 'Look' command groups.

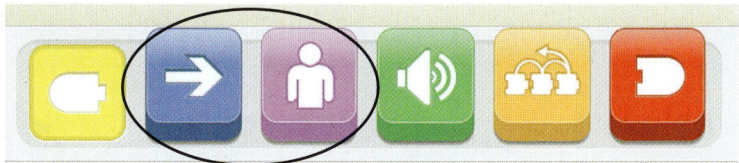

Join one command to the 'Start on green flag' trigger command. To do this, drag your command next to the green flag and join them together.

Then tap on the green flag at the top of the screen to run the program. Let's see what happens!

If you want to delete (get rid of) a command, you can:

- drag it away from the command it is joined to and move it to the right, or
- drag it back into the command group it came from.

Discuss with your partner what the commands do when they are run. What happens to the sprite?

How many commands can you look at? Can you add several commands together and run the program?

How am I doing?

Draw pictures of all the commands you have looked at on a piece of paper. Find someone with a different command to yours. Ask them to explain what it does.

You have started to learn what some of the commands in ScratchJr do. When we know what each command in ScratchJr does, it helps us to choose the correct ones when we make programs.

1 Computational thinking and programming

Unplugged activity 1

Matching

> You will need:
> a pencil and paper or a whiteboard pen and mini whiteboard

Look at the commands below. Can you match the pictures of the commands with the descriptions of what the commands do?

Write down which letter matches each number. I will do the first one for you: A = 2.

Command		Description
A		1 Moves the sprite one place to the right.
B		2 Makes the program run when the green flag is clicked.
C		3 Adds a speech bubble above the sprite.
D		4 Makes the sprite grow by one unit.
E		5 Makes the sprite move up one place and then down.
F		6 Makes the sprite go back to its starting place.

Making an animal animation in ScratchJr

Arun is now going to make a program in ScratchJr. He will use the snake and frog animation algorithm that you acted out earlier.

Here is the algorithm again to remind us:

1 Computational thinking and programming

Follow Arun's steps to make the first part of the program. (You will make the second part later.)

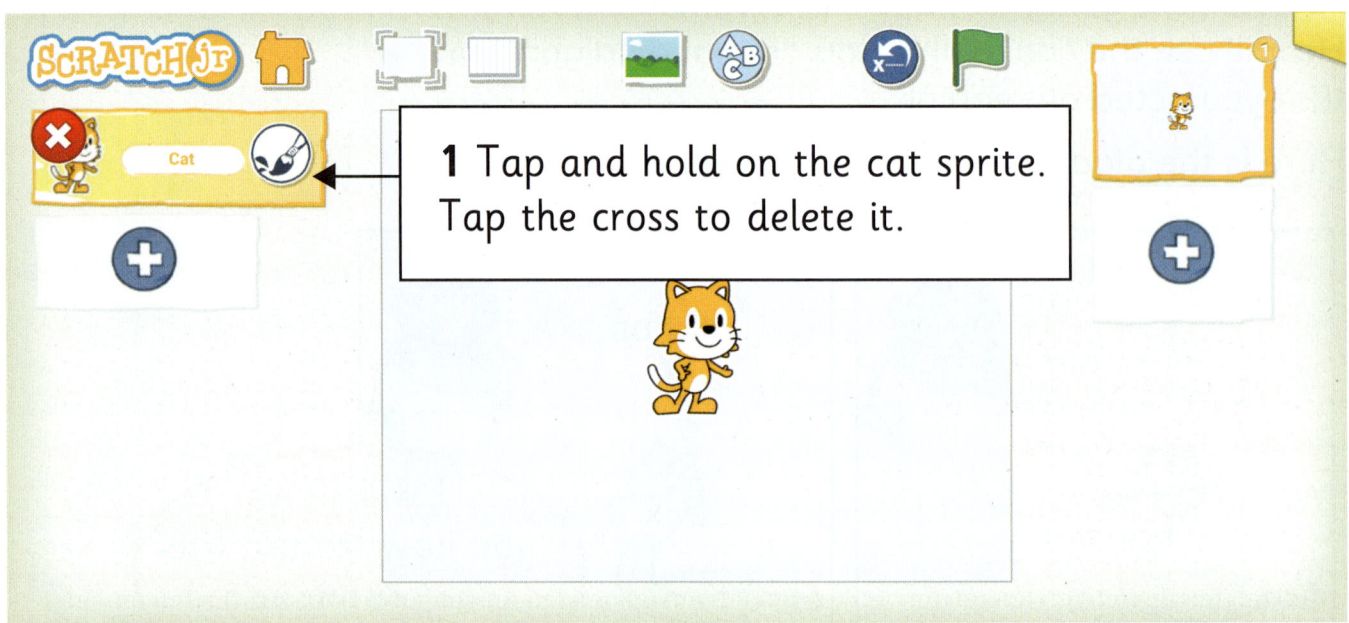

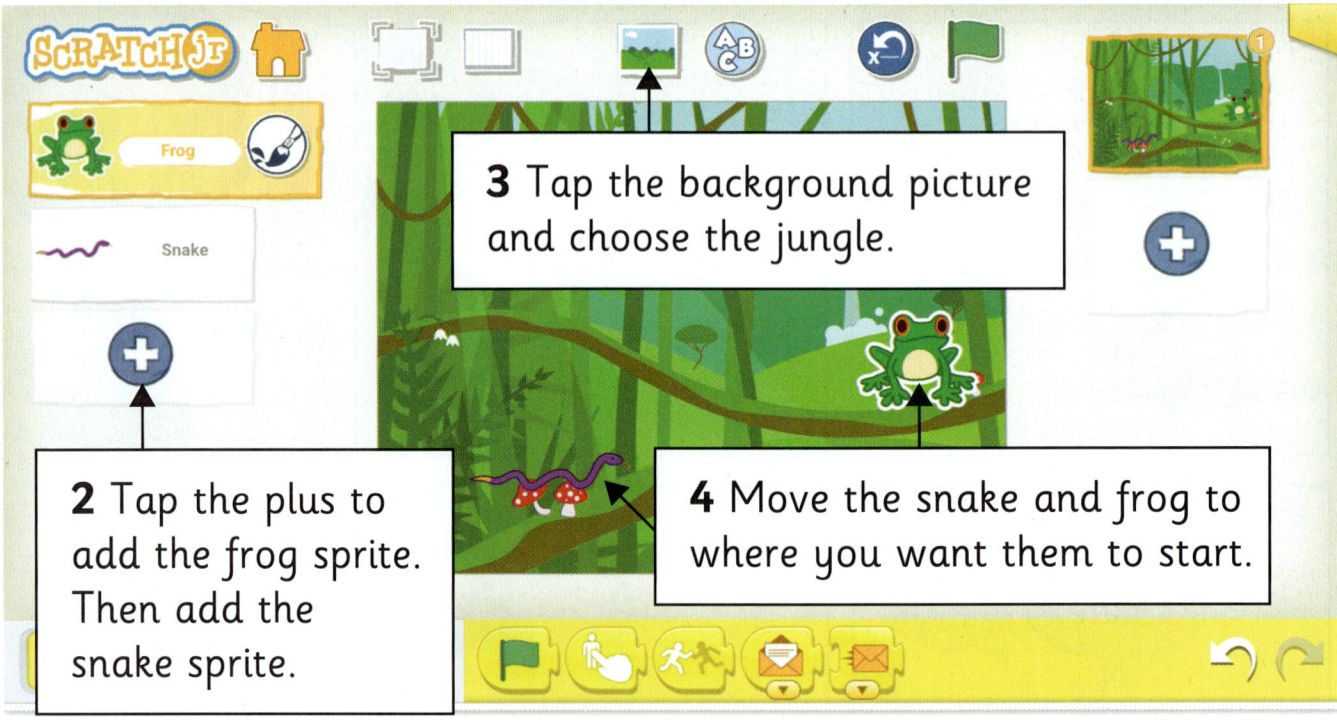

1.3 Animal animations

Now you have the sprites and background for your animation. Next, Arun will show you how to make the program.

I will explain the commands you need to turn this algorithm into a program.

Arun will add the commands to create the program for the frog. He checks the algorithm at the start of the section.

First, the frog sprite needs to say, 'I hop.' Then it needs to hop.

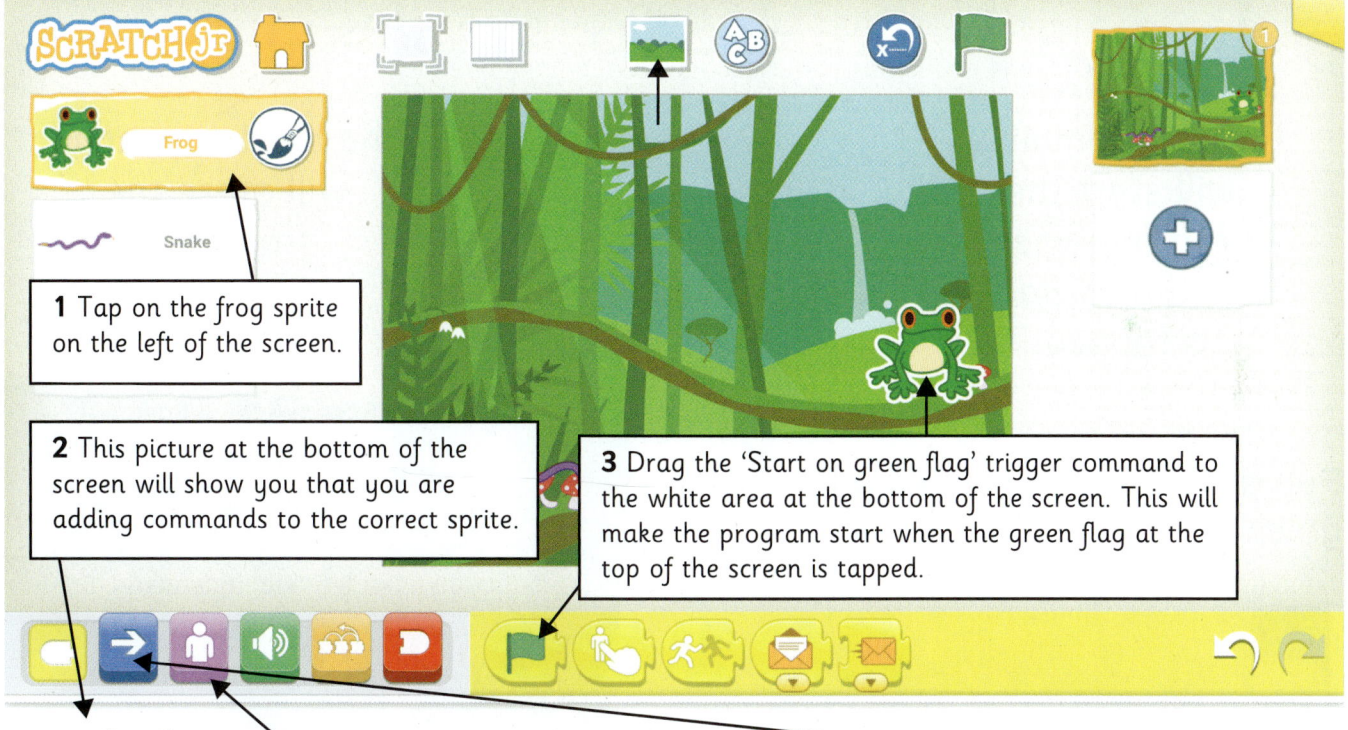

1 Tap on the frog sprite on the left of the screen.

2 This picture at the bottom of the screen will show you that you are adding commands to the correct sprite.

3 Drag the 'Start on green flag' trigger command to the white area at the bottom of the screen. This will make the program start when the green flag at the top of the screen is tapped.

4 Tap on the 'Looks' command group and find the 'Say' command. You can see what it looks like on the next page.

Drag the command into the white area and join it to the trigger command. To change the text in the 'Say' command, tap on it. Change the text to: 'I hop.'

5 Tap on the 'Motion' command group and find the 'Hop' command. You can see what it looks like on the next page.

Drag the command into the white area and join it to the other commands.

55

1 Computational thinking and programming

If you are not sure where to find a command, they are all grouped by colour.

The first command will start the program when the green flag is tapped.

The second command will add a speech bubble which says, 'I hop.'

The third command will make the frog hop.

Run the program by tapping the green flag at the top of the screen.

Can you see that Arun's program matches the algorithm for the frog?

1.3 Animal animations

Changing the number in commands

Arun's 'Hop' command had the number 2 underneath it:

What do you think will happen if you change the number to a larger number?

Try it and run the program to find out if you were right.

Changing the number to a larger number makes the frog hop higher!

Question

2 Discuss with a partner. What do you think will happen if you make the numbers bigger in the following commands?

a
1

b
1

c
2

1 Computational thinking and programming

Programming task 2

Finishing the animal animation

> You will need:
> a computer or tablet running ScratchJr

Work with a partner. Make the rest of the animal animation algorithm into a program.

Arun has shown you the commands for the frog sprite. Can you add the commands for the snake sprite?

The algorithm shows the snake should:

1. Move to the centre.
2. Say, 'I slide.'
3. Move to the right.

Remember to tap on the sprite you want to add the commands to.

What commands can you use to turn this part of the algorithm into code? Here are two top tips from Sofia to help you.

Sofia's first top tip

To make the snake move after the frog, you can use the 'Wait' command:

You will find this in the orange 'Control' command group:

Try exploring how long the snake has to wait by changing the number.

58

1.3 Animal animations

Continued

Sofia's second top tip

Use the 'Go home' command at the end of your program:

This will make sure the snake starts in the correct place when you run your program again.

You will find this in the 'Motion' command group:

Remember to use your debugging skills from Topic 1.2 to help you debug your program.

You can test (check) each step of your program. Run it each time you add a new command to make sure it is correct.

You can also talk through your program with your partner.

How are we doing?

Work with another pair. Run your programs to show each other your completed animation. Do they match the algorithm?

Compare which commands you have used. Discuss any differences.

1 Computational thinking and programming

Did you become more confident using ScratchJr during Topic 1.3?

Why do you think we get more confident the more we use something?

Look what I can do!
- ☐ I can follow an algorithm.
- ☐ I understand that programs tell computers how to run algorithms.
- ☐ I can turn an algorithm into a program in ScratchJr.

> 1.4 Repeat, repeat, repeat

We are going to:

- understand why repeat (doing something over and over) commands are used in programs
- learn how to use repeat commands in ScratchJr.

> algorithm   programming language
> code   repeat
> command   repeat command
> debug   run
> predict   ScratchJr
> program

Getting started

What do you already know?

- You learnt to use some ScratchJr commands.
- You turned an algorithm into a program.
- You debugged programs.

61

1 Computational thinking and programming

Continued

Now try this!

We looked at ScratchJr in Topic 1.3.

You can make objects and characters called sprites do lots of different things in ScratchJr.

Look at this program in ScratchJr.

 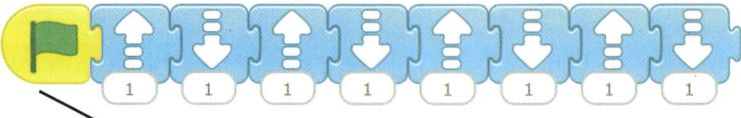

This is the program. It tells the sprite (cat) what to do.

Discuss with a partner.

1 What do you think the sprite will do when we run this ScratchJr program?

2 Do you see a pattern in the commands? Explain the pattern to your partner.

1.4 Repeat, repeat, repeat

Repeat commands

Sometimes the same commands are used over and over again in a program. We say the commands are repeated.

Programming languages like ScratchJr have special commands.

They tell the computer to repeat other commands. These are called repeat commands.

This is a repeat command from ScratchJr:

Repeat commands can make programs shorter. This can help us to read them and debug them.

Zara has used the repeat command to shorten the program from 'Now try this'.

Now it looks like this:

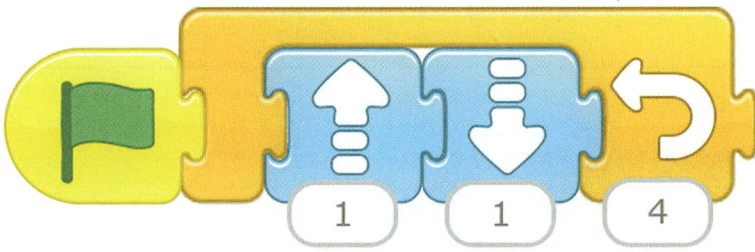

Questions

1 Can you point to the repeat command?
2 What do you think the number 4 means?

1 Computational thinking and programming

We will learn about two types of repeat command in this topic:

- repeat a certain number of times
- repeat forever.

Remember the colour of commands show which menu they are in. In ScratchJr, these commands look like this:

Repeat command	What it does
Repeat a certain number of times	Commands inside this command will be repeated the number of times shown. Here, it is set to 4, but we can change this.
Repeat forever	We can put this command at the end of a program. It will repeat the program over and over from the beginning. It will continue forever. Do not worry! We can still stop the program when we want by clicking the red hexagon:

We will learn about repeat commands in this topic. Repeating things can also help us to learn!

You might practise your multiplication tables over and over to remember them. What else do you repeat to get better at it?

1.4 Repeat, repeat, repeat

Unplugged activity 1

A flying sprite

You will need:
a pencil and paper or a whiteboard pen and mini whiteboard

Arun has made a program in ScratchJr.

He has used the two types of repeat command in his program.

Discuss with a partner. Predict what the plane will do when the program is run. You can write down your ideas, say them or draw them.

Do not worry if you find it hard to predict what this program will do. We will learn more about repeat commands in the rest of this topic.

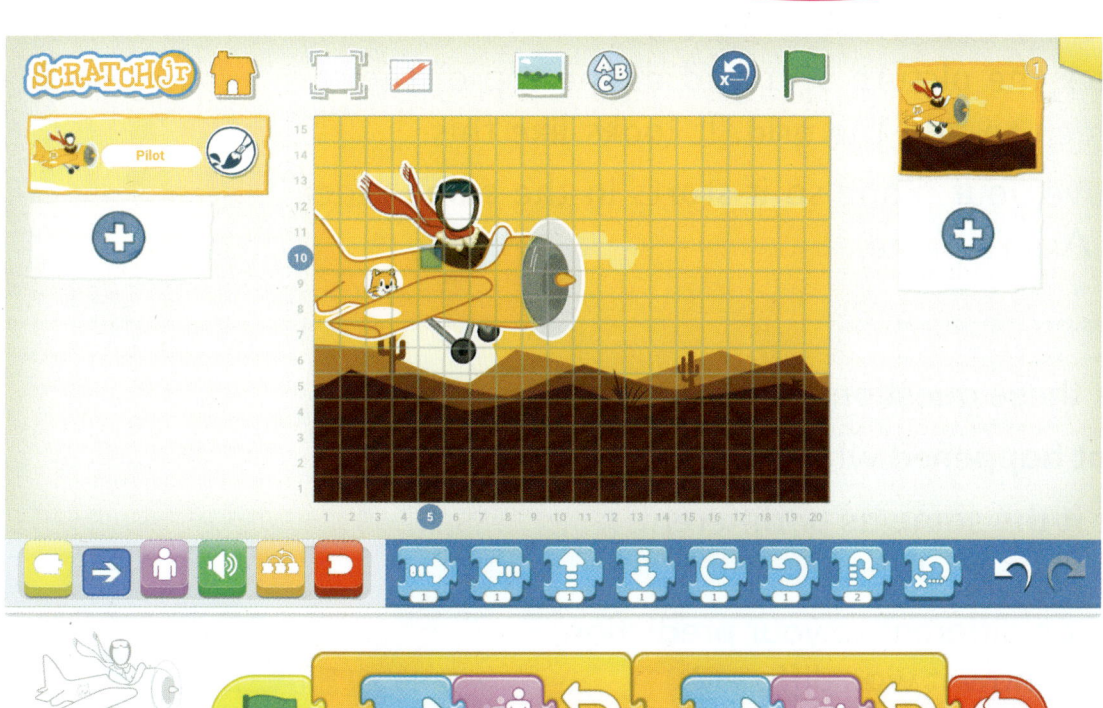

65

1 Computational thinking and programming

Programming task 1

What happens to the sprite?

> **You will need:**
> a computer or tablet running ScratchJr

You predicted what Arun's program will do when he runs it.

Make the program in ScratchJr. Then run it to see if it matches what you predicted.

Sofia has some top tips to help you.

Sofia's top tips

- You learnt how to change sprites and backgrounds in Topic 1.3. Look back if you cannot remember.
- Click the picture of a grid at the top of the screen to add the grid. It looks like this:
- Move your plane so it starts in the same place as Arun's plane.

Discuss these questions with a partner.

1 What happened when you ran your program?
2 Was it the same as or different from your prediction?
3 If it was different to your prediction, discuss how it was different.

1.4 Repeat, repeat, repeat

You tested whether your prediction was correct by making and running Arun's program. We will now find out more about the program.

We will learn more about the repeat commands.

Questions

Look at this program:

3. Can you point to the two 'Repeat a certain number of times' commands?

4. Which commands are repeated by each 'Repeat a certain number of times' command?

5. Can you point to the 'Repeat forever' command?

Now you will make some predictions about what will happen if you change this program.

To help predict what a program will do, trace your finger over each command.

Think about what it would do, just like you do when you are reading words in a book.

1 Computational thinking and programming

Programming task 2

ScratchJr challenges

> **You will need:**
> a computer or tablet running ScratchJr

Look at your program from Programming task 1 in ScratchJr. Complete these steps for each of the following challenges:

1 Make the change.
2 Predict what will happen when the program is run.
3 Run the program to see if you were correct.

Challenge 1: Remove the 'repeat forever' command from the end of your program, as shown here:

Challenge 2: Remove the second block of 'Repeat a certain number of times' commands from your program.

Replace it with the 'Repeat forever' command, as shown here:

Remember to make a prediction first, then run the program to check your prediction.

1.4 Repeat, repeat, repeat

Continued

Challenge 3: Change the number in the first repeat command to 6. Change the number in the second repeat command to 1, as shown here:

Challenge 4: Try to add another command in each repetition command.

An example is shown here but you can choose any command you like:

How am I doing?

Work with a partner. Choose one of the commands below and explain to your partner what it does and how you use it.

Your partner will explain the other command to you.

1 Computational thinking and programming

You have explored how repeat commands work. We will now change the program to make it do different things.

Programming task 3

Making more changes in ScratchJr

> You will need:
> a computer or tablet running ScratchJr

First, make Arun's original program in ScratchJr, shown here:

You will work with a partner for this task.
You learnt why it is useful to work with others in Topic 1.3.

Challenge 1: Can you make the program only run once and not repeat forever?

Challenge 2: Can you make the program keep repeating the command 'move one place to the right and grow by 2' forever?

Challenge 3: Can you make the plane grow and shrink by the same amount as the program runs? Start by rebuilding Arun's original program for this challenge.

1.4 Repeat, repeat, repeat

Did you know?

Some computer programmers work in pairs to make programs.

We call this pair programming. It helps them find bugs in their programs.

Why do you think working in pairs helps computer programmers to find bugs?

Can you think of some other reasons why it is good to work in pairs?

Look what I can do!

☐ I understand why repeat commands are used in programs.

☐ I can use repeat commands in ScratchJr.

1 Computational thinking and programming

Project

Make your own animation program in ScratchJr

> You will need:
> source file **1.3_planning_grid**, pens and pencils, a computer or tablet running ScratchJr

In this project, you will make your own ScratchJr animation. You will work in pairs.

Your animation should:

- have two sprites
- use commands in the 'Look' and 'Motion' command groups
- use repeat commands.

Part A is to plan your algorithm.
You will draw what you want your sprites to do.

Part B is to turn this algorithm into a program in ScratchJr.

Your animation can be about anything! Have a look at the sprites and backgrounds in ScratchJr first to help give you ideas.

1.4 Repeat, repeat, repeat

Continued

Part A: Plan your algorithm

First, choose your background in ScratchJr and then choose two sprites. Use these in the plan that you will now write.

Plan your animation by drawing it in four squares.

Your teacher will give you a grid for this. Add notes to show:

- how your sprite will move
- what they will say
- how they willl change size.

Include some repetition. This can be repeating movements or speech.

1 Computational thinking and programming

Continued

Sofia is using the girl and basketball sprites with the basketball court background. Here is a plan that Sofia made:

The child starts on the left and moves to the right.

The child says: 'I love basketball.'

The child says: 'I will practise.'

The ball moves up and down four times.

1.4 Repeat, repeat, repeat

Continued

Part B: Turn your algorithm into a program

Make your algorithm into a program in ScratchJr.

Show your animation programs to your class. Explain which part of the program you found the most difficult to make and why.

Explain any errors that you found and then debugged.

Remember to use your debugging skills. Keep testing your program!

1 Computational thinking and programming

Check your progress

1 Why should an algorithm be precise?

  A To make it longer.

  B To make sure you get the correct result.

  C To make it easier to remember.

2 Which of these algorithms for a Bee-Bot will draw a square?

  A

  B

  C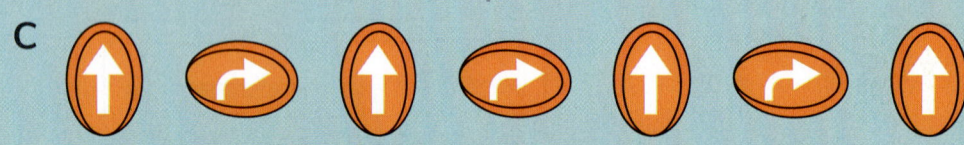

3 Write down **one** top tip to help debug programs.

4 Complete the sentence. ScratchJr is…

  A a programming language

  B an object or character we can move in a program

  C a computer game.

5 Marcus is making a program in ScratchJr. He wants his sprite to grow.

  Which command should Marcus use?

  A    B    C

Continued

6 Sofia has made a simple program. She wants her program to repeat over and over forever.

Which repeat command should Sofia use?

A  B  C

7 Arun is making a program in ScratchJr.

His sprite needs to move up two squares, then shrink by two. It needs to repeat this three times.

Which program should Arun use?

A

B

C

2 > Managing data

> ## 2.1 Data all around

We are going to:
- find out why we use a computer to store data
- look at different types of data
- record different types of data.

collect	password
data	personal data
form	record
organise	store

Getting started

What do you already know?

- A piece of data is a fact. It can be a word, number or picture.
- Computers can sort and organise data.
- We can ask questions to help collect data.
- We can use a form to enter data into a computer.

Now try this!

Copy this table. Complete the table to show the data for your country.

You can use the internet to find the information you need.

Your teacher will show you a website.

Country name	Name of the capital city	A picture of the flag

2.1 Data all around

Organising data

A computer can help us to **organise** data. Organise means to put things in an order that makes sense.

When **data** is organised in a table on the computer, it helps us find the information we are looking for.

Now you are going to organise data into a table.

Activity 1

What should I wear?

> You will need:
> a desktop computer, laptop or tablet with internet access, source file **2.1_weather_clothing**

Your teacher will give you the file for this activity.

Think about the clothes you would wear in different weathers. Organise the clothes into the correct section of the table.

Use the mouse to drag and drop the pieces of clothing.

When you have organised all the pictures, think of one more thing to add to each section.

How am I doing?

Find a partner. Look at their answers. Are they the same or different?

What ideas did you both have for one more thing to add to each section?

79

2 Managing data

Storing data

Sometimes we want to **store** data. Store means to keep the data so we can use it again.

We can store data in different ways. The photos all show things that can store data.

Point to the computers you can see. Say their names.

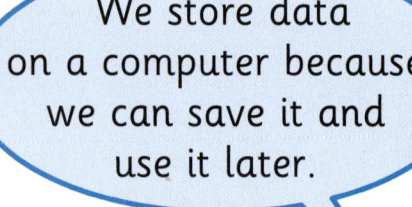

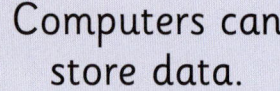
Computers can store data.

We store data on a computer because we can save it and use it later.

Storing data on a computer also keeps it safe and means it is less likely to get lost.

2.1 Data all around

Data at the doctor's surgery

Schools, shops and banks all store data.
Your doctor stores data about you, such as:

- your name
- your age
- any medical problems you have.

This data is all stored on a computer.

The doctor's computer stores each person's data in a **record**. A record keeps all the data together for each person.

Max's record looks like this on the doctor's computer screen.

Name	Age	Problem
Max Wilson	6	Ear infection

Question

1. What other examples of computers storing data can you think of? Discuss with a partner.

My games console stores data about who got the highest score.

2 Managing data

Unplugged activity 2

In the doctor's waiting room

> You will need:
> a pencil and paper or a whiteboard pen and mini whiteboard

This table shows the data of all the patients (people who need medical help) in the doctor's waiting room.

Name	Age	Problem
Max Wilson	6	ear infection
Jamila Rasheed	12	cough
Lemar Carter	35	headache
Freya Perry	3	cough
Zainab Shamu	21	broken leg

Use the table to answer these questions about the data.

1 How many patients are under 10 years old?
2 How many people have a cough?
3 How many patients are at the doctor's altogether?

2.1 Data all around

If data is mixed up, it can be hard to understand.

Think how difficult it would be to find books in a library if they were not in alphabetical (A–Z) order by author.

We would need to organise the books first so that the order made sense to us. Then we could find things easily.

We can do the same thing with data that is on a computer.

2 Managing data

Activity 3

At the vet

> **You will need:**
> a desktop computer, laptop or tablet with internet access, source file **2.2_animal_table**

The vet has lots of animals to care for today. She is worried that she might not have enough medicine to make them all better.

The vet decides to use a computer to organise and store the data about her animals.

If she keeps today's data, it might help her to know how much medicine to buy on other days.

Help the vet to count the animals and organise them in the table. Your teacher will give you a table to help you.

2.1 Data all around

> **Continued**
>
> Use your table to answer these questions:
>
> 1 Which animal does the vet have the most of?
>
> 2 Which animal does the vet have the fewest of?
>
> 3 How many animals are there in total?

Keeping data safe

There are other reasons why we keep data on a computer.

Some data is private, like doctors' records. It needs to be kept safe. Computers help to keep our data safe.

When private data is stored on a computer, a **password** is used to protect it.

A password is set of letters, numbers and symbols.

Only people who know the password will be able to see the data.

They will keep the password secret to keep the data safe.

> **Stay safe!**
>
> Be careful if you are asked to type in **personal data** on the internet. This is information that you should keep private, such as your full name, where you live, your date of birth.
>
> You need to know who can see your personal data. Always check with a trusted adult first.

2 Managing data

How to store data

There are 100 children in Zara's sports club. She wants to find out what the most popular sport is.

She asks each child to write their favourite sport on a piece of paper and give it back to her.

When we have lots of data, it is easier to use a computer.

Zara decides to send the children a **form** on the computer instead. A form is something that has questions on it that a person can answer. Now their answers will go straight into the computer and be saved there.

This is going to take too long!

2.1 Data all around

The next day, Zara wants to check how many people have tennis as their favourite sport.

As she stored the data on a computer, she can use the data again.

Activity 4

Why store data?

> You will need:
> a pencil and paper or a whiteboard pen and mini whiteboard,
> source file **2.3_storing_data**

Your teacher will give you a file for this activity.

Look at the different types of data that need to be stored on a computer.

Why should this data be stored on a computer? Put them in the correct place in the table.

- 1000 words for children to learn
- bank account details
- a child's school records
- a list of all the books in a bookshop
- your friend's phone number
- a record of the daily temperature from the last ten years

87

2 Managing data

Before we **collect** (get) data, we think about what we want to find out.

First, we look at the question we are trying to answer. Then we decide what data to collect.

Unplugged activity 5

Counting colours

You will need:
a pencil and paper or a whiteboard pen and mini whiteboard

I have a jar of coloured counters. I want to know which colour counter I have most of.

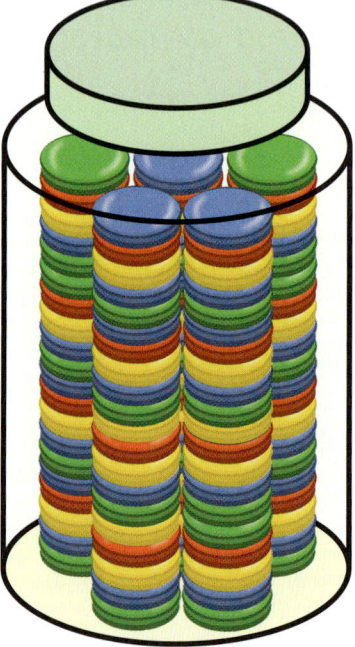

Talk to a partner. Discuss what data Sofia needs to collect.

How could she do this? Write down your ideas.

2.1 Data all around

Now it's your turn! You are going to collect your own data.

> **Practical task 1**
>
> **Collect your own data**
>
> > You will need:
> > a desktop computer, laptop or tablet with internet access, source file **2.4_collecting_data**
>
>
>
> Think about something you would like to find out from your classmates. Here are some things you could ask them about:
>
> - number of siblings (brothers and sisters)
> - what pets they have
> - favourite film.
>
> Think about how you are going to collect the data. What question are you going to ask?
>
> Next, collect the data from ten learners. Use a computer and add your data to a table that your teacher will give you.
>
> You can change the heading to fit your idea. Your teacher will show you how to save your table.
>
> Discuss with a partner:
>
> 1. What type of data have you collected? Have you collected words, numbers or pictures? Or a mix?
>
> > I collected their names which are in words. Their answer was about how many pets they have so this was in numbers.
>
>
>
> 2. What would you do if someone wanted to change their answer next week? How does the data being stored on a computer help with this?

2 Managing data

Did you know?

There are lots of big collections of data on the internet. You might have used some of them! Websites like Google or YouTube are some of the biggest collections of data in the world.

In this topic, you have organised some data so that it makes sense.

If you find something confusing, what do you do so that it makes sense? Explain your answer.

Look what I can do!

- [ ] I can say why we use a computer to store data.
- [ ] I know that there are different types of data.
- [ ] I can record different types of data.

> 2.2 Problem solvers

We are going to:
- learn about the difference between statistical and non-statistical questions
- answer questions using different types of data
- use data to solve problems.

non-statistical question

statistical question

Getting started

What do you already know?
- There are different types of data.
- You can record different types of data.
- You understand why computers are used to store (keep) data.

2 Managing data

Continued

Now try this!

Arun asked three of his friends a question. Here are their answers:

 hide and seek skipping hopscotch

What question do you think Arun asked?

A What is your favourite colour?

B What is your favourite game?

C What is your favourite fruit?

When we want to find information, we have to ask the right questions to help us find the answer.

2.2 Problem solvers

Types of questions

Sometimes a question can only have one answer.

We call this a **non-statistical question**.

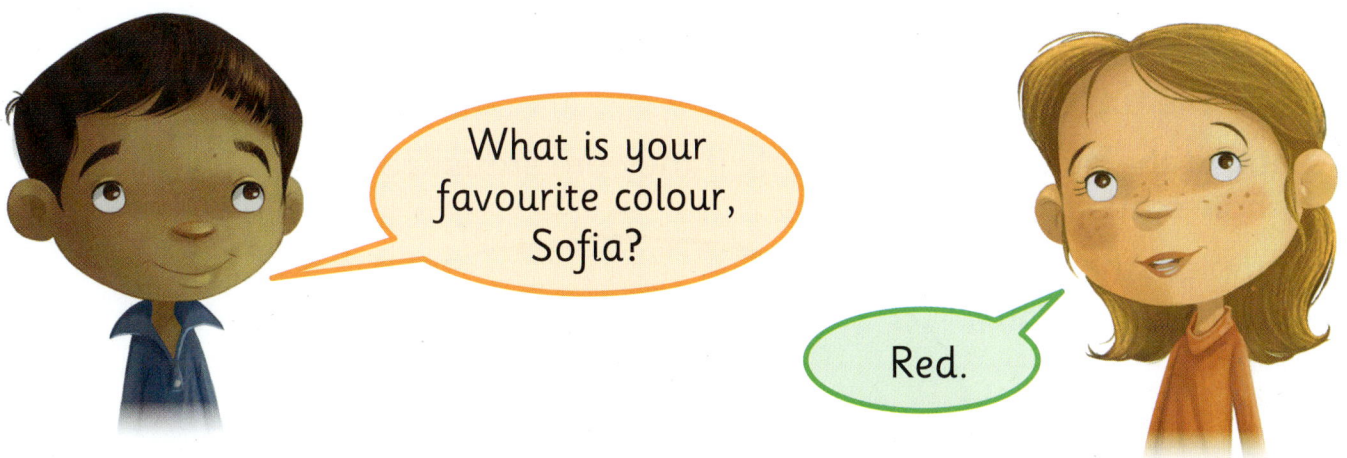

What is your favourite colour, Sofia?

Red.

Sometimes we need to collect data to answer a question.

We call this a **statistical question**.

What is the favourite colour of everyone in my class?

2 Managing data

Unplugged activity 1

Which type of question?

> You will need:
> a pencil and paper or a whiteboard pen and mini whiteboard

Copy the table below.

Look at the questions and decide if they are statistical or non-statistical.

Complete the table by putting a tick in the correct column.

Remember, we need to collect data to answer statistical questions. Non-statistical questions only have one answer.

Question	Statistical	Non-statistical
What size are your shoes?		
What is the most common shoe size in our class?		
What is your favourite flavour of ice cream?		
What is the most popular flavour of ice cream in our school?		

If you want an extra challenge, you could say whether the data is usually words, numbers or pictures.

Answering a statistical question

To answer a statistical question, we can collect data.

Zara is going to collect her own statistical data.

Zara's teacher has said the class can plan a class treat for working so hard all week.

The problem is that the class has lots of ideas but can't agree which one to choose.

The teacher asks Zara to help him find out what the most popular idea is.
How can Zara collect everyone's ideas?

Say or write down some questions she could ask her classmates. Share your ideas with a partner.

2 Managing data

Zara decides to let her classmates vote by choosing one of these ideas:

- play board games
- play sports
- watch a film.

Zara counts the votes.

She makes this table on her tablet.

Activity	Number of votes
play board games	10
play sports	4
watch a film	11

Questions

1. Which was the most popular idea?
2. Which was the least popular idea?
3. Look at the data in the 'Number of votes' column. Is it pictures, words or numbers?
4. What do you think about the way Zara collected the data?

Zara needed to collect statistical data to answer the question. The data helped her to solve (sort out, or fix) a problem.

Now it is your turn to collect statistical data to solve a problem.

Practical task 1

What's for lunch?

You will need:
a pencil and paper or a whiteboard pen and mini whiteboard, a desktop computer, laptop or tablet, source file **2.5_lunch_choices**

Imagine that your class is having a special lunch to celebrate the end of term.

The school cook is making three meals:

- pasta
- pizza
- chicken and rice.

The cook has a problem. He wants to make sure everyone gets their favourite lunch, but he does not know how much of each meal to cook.

2 Managing data

> **Continued**
>
> Can you help the cook by collecting data from your classmates?
>
> What question will you ask them? Write it down.
>
> Decide how you will record their choices.
>
> Collect the data by holding a class vote.
>
> Once you have collected the data, use your tablet or computer to put the data into the table that your teacher will give you.
>
> Look at your data. Does it give you the information you need to tell the cook what to make?
>
> **How am I doing?**
>
> Compare your answer with a partner's answer. Did their table look the same as yours?
>
> Was it easy to get the information that the cook needed?

2.2 Problem solvers

Unplugged activity 2

Books, books, books!

> You will need:
> a pencil and paper or a whiteboard pen and mini whiteboard

Marcus's teacher is choosing some new books for the class reading area.

She doesn't know which kinds of stories to buy, so she asks Marcus to collect some data to find out which will be popular.

This is the data he collected.

funny stories	12
scary stories	15
animal stories	6

1   Which question do you think Marcus asked?

   A   Who likes stories?

   B   What is your favourite type of story?

   C   Who is the author of this story?

2   Which type of book should Marcus's teacher buy the most of?

3   Which type of book should Marcus's teacher buy the fewest of?

2 Managing data

Did you know?

When we take a digital photo, data about the photo is stored with it.

The data can include details on when and where the photo was taken.

It might even include which camera was used to take the photo!

You have learnt about collecting data to help solve problems.

Do you have any ways of solving problems more easily?

Share them with a partner.

Look what I can do!

- ☐ I understand the difference between statistical and non-statistical questions.
- ☐ I can answer questions using different types of data.
- ☐ I can use data to solve problems.

> 2.3 Presenting data

We are going to:
- collect data to help answer a question
- find out about different types of graphs and charts
- make graphs and charts from our data.

> block graph   pictogram
> form   present
> graph

Getting started

What do you already know?
- You can ask statistical or non-statistical questions to collect data.
- Data can help us to solve problems.

Now try this!

Sofia wants to find out which fruit juice is the most popular in her school. She asks Arun to help her collect the data.

2 Managing data

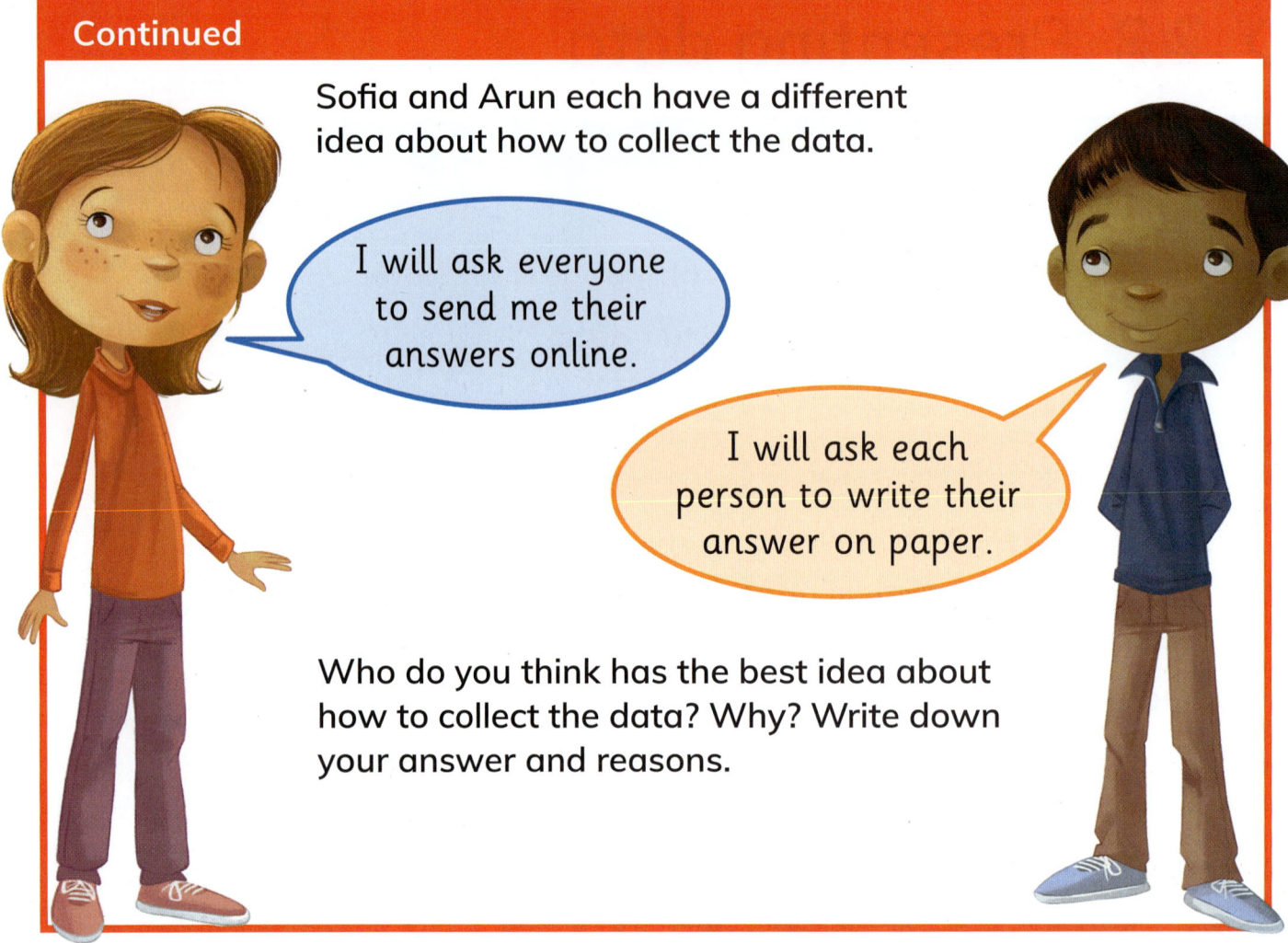

> **Continued**
>
> Sofia and Arun each have a different idea about how to collect the data.
>
> "I will ask everyone to send me their answers online."
>
> "I will ask each person to write their answer on paper."
>
> Who do you think has the best idea about how to collect the data? Why? Write down your answer and reasons.

Collecting data

If we want to collect data from lots of people, it can take a long time to ask every person and write down their answer.

Using a form on a computer can help us. Remember, a form is something that has questions on it that a person can answer.

Lots of people can add their data to a form at the same time, so it is quicker.

Data we collect using a form is saved on the computer. This keeps it safe and means that we can use it later.

Now you are going to use a form to add your own data.

2.3 Presenting data

> **Activity 1**
>
> **Favourite flavours**
>
> > You will need:
> > a desktop computer, laptop or tablet with internet access, online form **2.6_flavour_form**
>
> Zara is planning an ice-cream stall for her school's summer fair. She wants to know how much of each ice cream to buy.
>
> Your teacher will give you Zara's form so you can add your choice.

Which of these ice-cream flavours do you like best?

Using lists

In the form you completed, you chose from a list of ice-cream flavours.

Giving people a list of choices means that they don't have to write the words.

This means there won't be any spelling mistakes. If there are spelling mistakes in the data, it can make it difficult to understand.

Presenting data

Once we have collected data, we can use a computer to **present** (show) it. The way we present data can help us to understand it.

When we see data as a **graph**, we can understand it more quickly and easily than looking at a list. Graphs are pictures that show data using lines, shapes or colours.

103

2 Managing data

A **block graph** shows data as blocks. Talk to a partner. Have you seen a block graph before? What data did it show?

What do you think this block graph is about? You can look at the title and the labels to help.

Zara wants to make a block graph to present her data from her ice-cream flavour form.

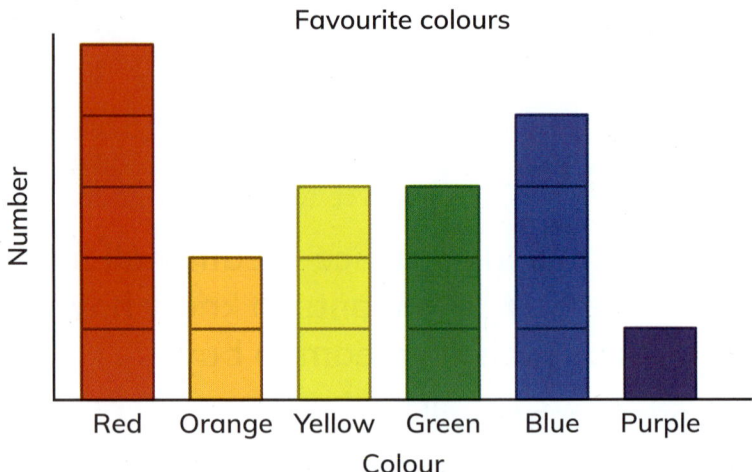

Activity 2

Make a graph!

You will need:
a desktop computer, laptop or tablet with internet access, data presentation software

Zara sends the form to her class. This is the data she collects:

Flavour	How many people chose it
chocolate	6
vanilla	5
strawberry	3
mint	2
caramel	4

Can you use the data in Zara's table to make your own block graph?

Your teacher will show you how to make a block graph on a computer.

104

2.3 Presenting data

Continued

Look at your block graph and answer these questions.

1. Which flavour is the most popular?
2. Which flavour is the least popular?
3. How many people chose caramel?
4. How many people did Zara ask altogether?

Thanks! Now I know how much of each flavour to buy!

How am I doing?

Compare your block graph to a partner's block graph.

Draw a star for your partner if they look the same.
If they look different, work together to find any errors.

2 Managing data

Pictograms

A **pictogram** is a different type of graph. It uses a picture to show each object that has been counted.

Unplugged activity 3

Favourite fruits

Marcus asked his friends what their favourite fruits are. He made a pictogram to show their answers.

In this pictogram, each picture shows one person's favourite fruit.

Apple	🍏	🍏	🍏	🍏	🍏	
Banana	🍌	🍌				
Orange	🍊					
Pear	🍐	🍐	🍐			
Strawberry	🍓	🍓	🍓	🍓	🍓	🍓

Sometimes the pictures go from the bottom to the top, and sometimes they go left to right – it means the same thing!

106

2.3 Presenting data

Continued

Look at the pictogram and answer these questions.

1. Which fruit is the most popular?
2. Which fruit is the least popular?
3. How many people like bananas?
4. How many friends did Marcus ask altogether?

How are we doing?

Talk to a partner about using the pictogram to answer the questions. Was it easy to use?

Did you know?

Sometimes we use pictures and words together to show and explain information.

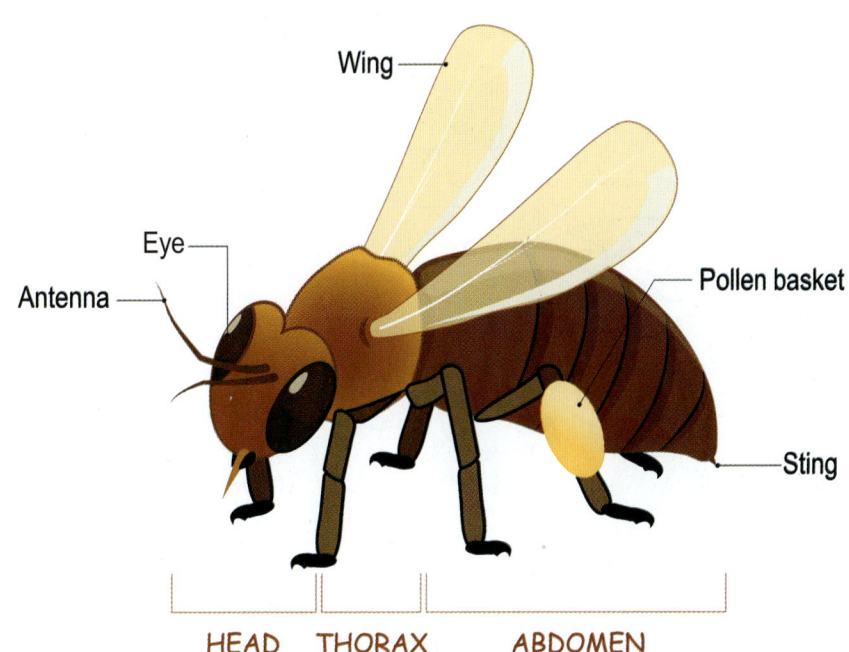

Worker honey bee

107

2 Managing data

Now you are going to collect data and present it in a pictogram.

Practical task 1

Minibeast hunt

You will need:
a pencil and paper or a whiteboard pen and mini whiteboard, a desktop computer, laptop or tablet with internet access, source file **2.7_minibeast_hunt** (optional), data presentation software

Sofia wants to know which minibeast (insect or spider) there is the most of in her garden.

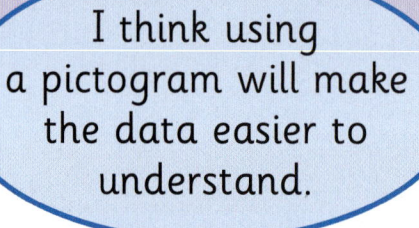

I think using a pictogram will make the data easier to understand.

Count the minibeasts in the picture above and help to make Sofia's pictogram. Your teacher will give you a table to fill in.

2.3 Presenting data

Continued

Now that you have collected your data, it is time to present it.

Your teacher will show you how to make a pictogram on a computer.

Look at your pictogram and write down the answers to these questions.

1. Which minibeast is there most of?
2. How many spiders did Sofia find?
3. Are there any minibeasts which she found the same number of?

How am I doing?

Compare your pictogram and answers with those of a partner. How easy did you find it to create the pictogram?

Do you think Sofia was right when she said that the data would be easier to understand as a pictogram? Why?

2 Managing data

Ways to show the same data

We present data in different ways. The table and block graph below show the same data.

Do you prefer the table or the block graph?
Do you find one easier to understand?
Discuss it with a partner.

Subject	Number of learners who like it best
Maths	3
English	2
Science	4
Art	3
Computing	6
History	3

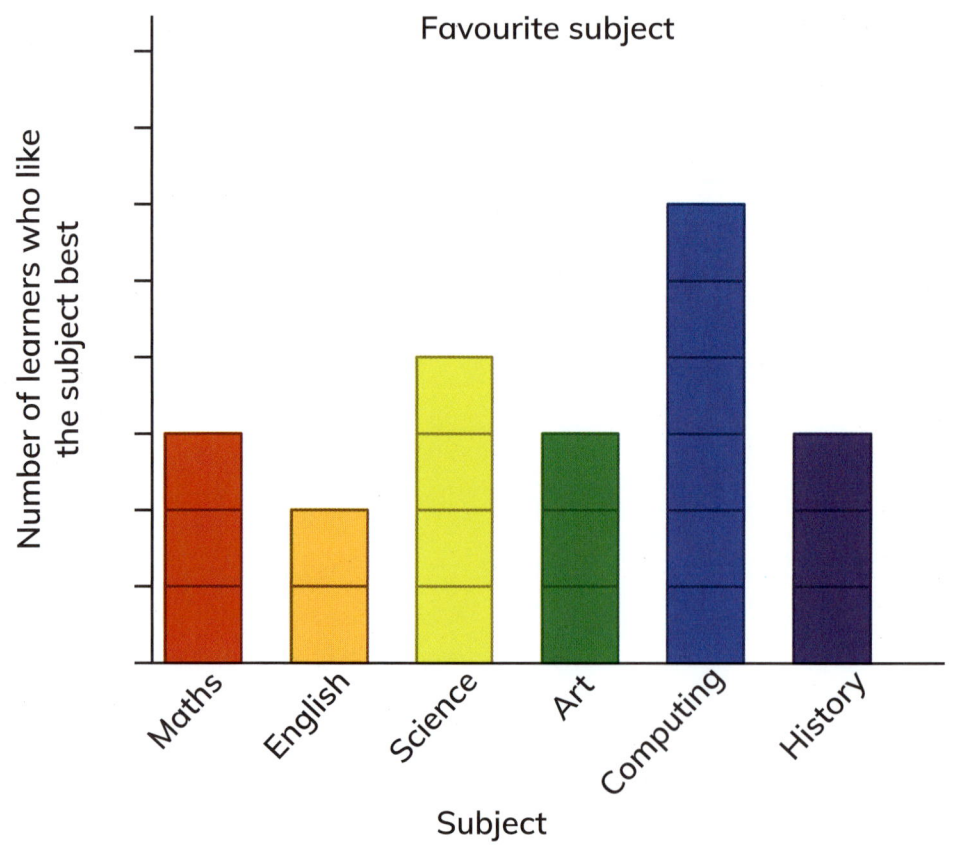

2.3 Presenting data

Look what I can do!

☐ I can collect data to help answer a question.

☐ I know about different types of graphs and charts.

☐ I can use data to make graphs and charts.

Project

Choosing clubs

You will need:
a desktop computer, laptop or tablet with internet access, source file **2.8_choosing_clubs**, data presentation software

Imagine that the headteacher at your school is planning which clubs to have next year.

Clubs are activities that you might do with other children in lunch breaks or after school.

> You could give them choices such as dancing, singing, acting, chess, sports.

Your headteacher does not know which clubs would be popular (liked and enjoyed by people). You can help the headteacher by collecting data from some people in your class.

Follow the steps below to help you solve the problem.

Step 1: What should you ask?

Think about what data you need to find.

- What question will you ask?
- Will you give people a list of clubs to choose from?

111

2 Managing data

> **Continued**
>
> **Step 2:** Collect your data.
>
> Imagine that your headteacher only wants you to find out what some learners think. The headteacher tells you to only ask 10 learners.
>
> Collect your data. Use the table that your teacher will give you.
>
> **Step 3:** Present your data.
>
> Make a graph to show your data. You can use a pictogram or a block graph.
>
> Your teacher will help you to do this.
>
> - Add your data to the graph.
> - Then add a title to your graph.
>
> Look at your graph and answer these questions.
>
> 1 Which club or clubs would be the most popular?
>
> 2 Which club or clubs would be the least popular?

2.3 Presenting data

Check your progress

1. Why do we use passwords?
2. Which of these questions would have an answer in numbers?

    A What is your favourite book?

    B What is your shoe size?

    C Do you like watching cartoons?

3. Describe the difference between a statistical question and a non-statistical question.
4. Which sort of question could you solve by collecting data? Statistical or non-statistical?
5. This is one of the questions on Zara's form: 'What is your favourite subject at school?'

    What choices would you give people for this question?

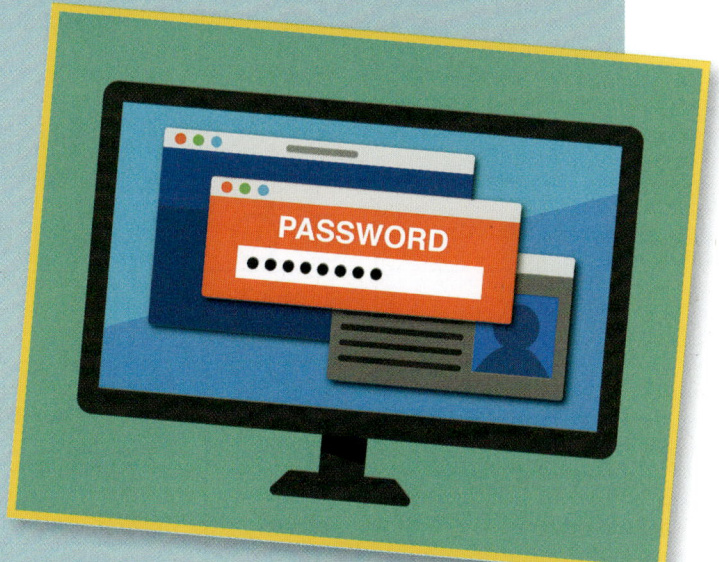

2 Managing data

Continued

6 This pictogram shows how people in Sofia's class travel to school.

How many people take the bus to school?

Bike	🚲	🚲	🚲			
Bus	🚌	🚌				
Car	🚗	🚗	🚗	🚗		
Walking	👟	👟	👟	👟	👟	👟

7 a What kind of graph is this?

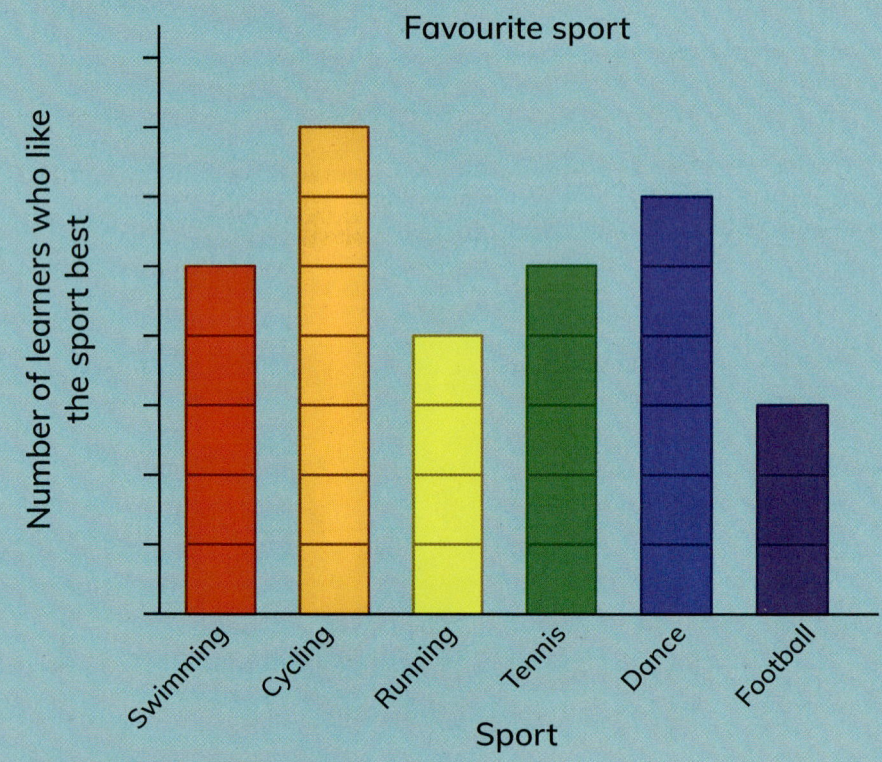

b Which is the most popular sport in this class?

c Which is the least popular sport in this class?

3 Networks and digital communication

> 3.1 Connect to a network

We are going to:
- find out which digital devices can connect to a network
- understand that there are wired and wireless networks
- learn when a network is and is not available.

available
connect
digital device
network
network cable
password
router
settings
wi-fi
wired connection
wireless connection

Getting started

What do you already know?
- We make a network by connecting several computers.
- Some computers connect to a network with wires.
- Some computers connect to a network without wires.
- The internet is a network of computers that are connected around the world.

115

3 Networks and digital communication

Continued

Now try this!

Do you use any digital devices at home?

A digital device is a piece of equipment which has a computer and does a task or number of tasks.

Draw a picture of a digital device you use at home.

Does your device have any of these parts?
If it does, add labels to your picture.

- touchscreen
- 'on' button
- 'home' button
- volume control
- place to plug in the charger
- place to plug in headphones

Does your digital device connect to (join) the internet?
How do you know?

3.1 Connect to a network

What connects to the internet at home?

Look at this picture.
Can you find three digital devices?

These digital devices can all connect to (join) the internet. When we use digital devices to connect to the internet, we can:

- find information
- watch videos
- listen to music
- message our friends.

What do you like to do on the internet?

What connects to the internet outside the home?

Schools, offices and shops all have their own networks.

Remember, a network is two or more computers that are joined together. Lots of digital devices are connected to these networks.

When the digital devices are connected to networks, they can share information easily.

117

3 Networks and digital communication

Arun and Sofia are in a supermarket. They can see some digital devices that can connect to a network.

The tills are connected to a network.

The scanners are connected to a network.

3.1 Connect to a network

Unplugged activity 1

At the supermarket

> You will need:
> a pencil and paper or a whiteboard pen and mini whiteboard

Look at this picture. It has some more digital devices that can connect to a network. Match them to the labels below the picture.

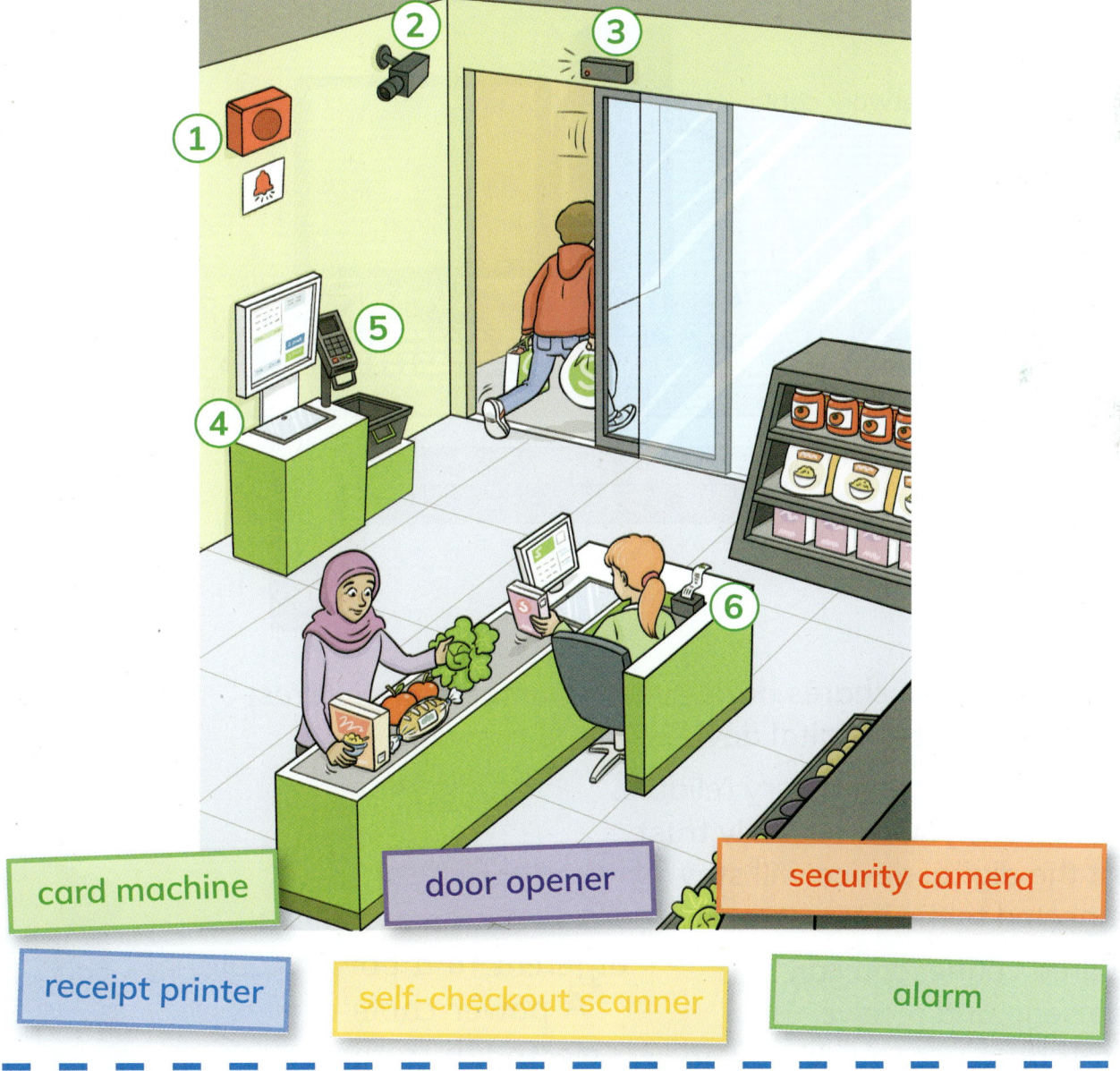

card machine   door opener   security camera

receipt printer   self-checkout scanner   alarm

3 Networks and digital communication

Wired connections

Digital devices like desktop computers connect to the internet using a **wired connection**.

Wired connections are joined together by wires. The wires are called **network cables**. The **router** is a device that sends data between computer networks.

It is an important part of a computer network.

We can see a wired connection below.

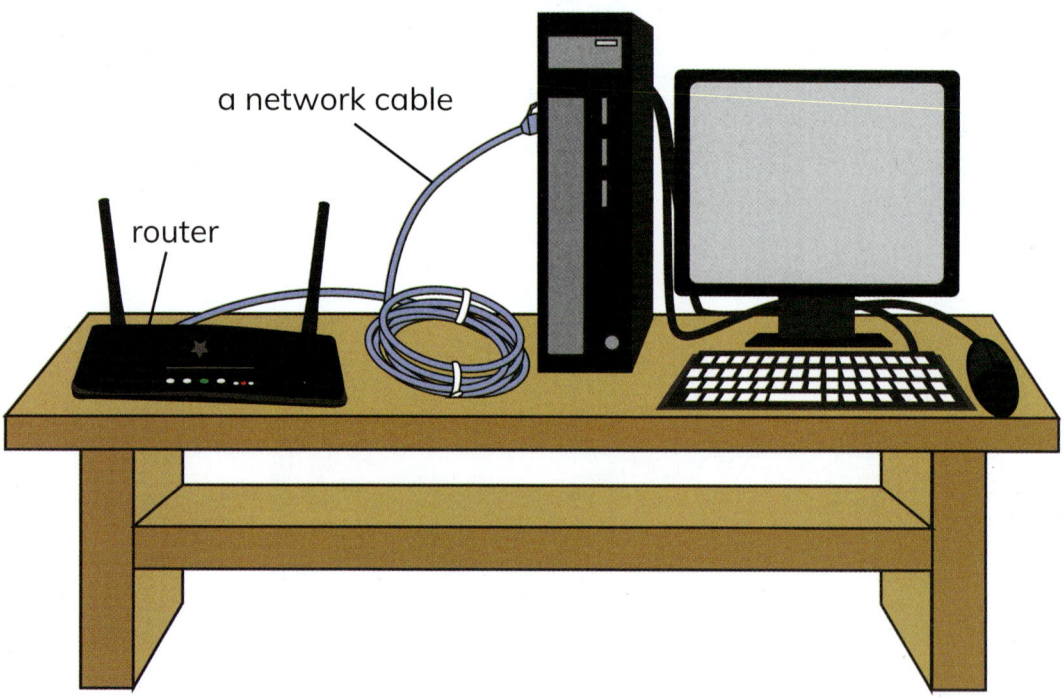

a network cable

router

A network cable shares data (words, numbers or pictures) between different digital devices on the network.

A wired connection is very reliable. That means you can usually trust that the digital device will stay connected to the internet.

A wired connection can also send and receive lots of data very quickly.

> A network cable is different to a power cable. A power cable carries electricity to the device so it can work.

120

3.1 Connect to a network

Wireless connections

Some digital devices use a **wireless connection**. They connect to a network without using a network cable.

A tablet and a phone are examples of wireless digital devices. We often call this type of connection a **wi-fi** connection.

When we use a wi-fi connection, we don't have to keep the digital device plugged into a network.

We can see a wireless connection below.

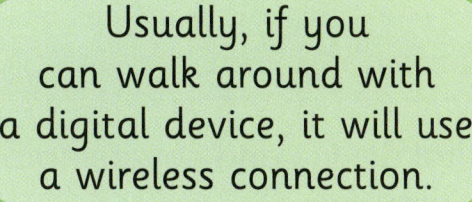
Usually, if you can walk around with a digital device, it will use a wireless connection.

121

3 Networks and digital communication

Unplugged activity 2

With or without wires?

> You will need:
> a pencil and paper or a whiteboard pen and mini whiteboard

Point to each digital device and say its name. They can all connect to the network.

Do they use a wired connection to do this, or a wireless connection (wi-fi)?

From the options, circle which type of connection each digital device uses.

Some can use both. The first one has been done for you.

1    (wired) / (wireless)

2    wired / wireless

3    wired / wireless

3.1 Connect to a network

Continued

4  wired / wireless

5  wired / wireless

6  wired / wireless

7  wired / wireless

How am I doing?

Which digital devices did you find that were wireless? Compare your answers with those of a partner.

3 Networks and digital communication

Problems connecting to a network

We have looked at different ways of connecting to a network. Sometimes, there can be problems connecting to a network. This can happen with wired or wireless connections.

Zara cannot connect to a network.

Things may not work if she is not connected to a network. Zara cannot:

- watch a film
- play a game on a website
- send a message to her friends using the internet
- make a video call to her family in another country.

3.1 Connect to a network

Let's look at some reasons why Zara cannot connect to the internet.

There might be a problem with the router.

The tablet might be too far away from the router to connect using wi-fi.

There might be a problem with the internet access.

Where can I connect to the internet?

Some places have better internet access than others.

Places where more people live and work have more networks that data can be shared through.

3 Networks and digital communication

Question

1 In which of these places could it be hard to connect to the internet? Compare your answers with those of a partner. Explain your choices.

Available networks

Available means something is ready for us to use.

We can see which wi-fi networks are available on our device by looking at the wi-fi **settings**. The settings on a digital device let us choose how it works.

You can see the wi-fi settings when you tap this button on the device's screen:

3.1 Connect to a network

The settings will show you which networks are available to join.

Stay safe!

Connecting to a network that you do not know can be dangerous.

Always check with an adult before connecting your digital device to a new network.

If you see this: next to a network, it means the network is locked. You need to type in a password to unlock the network. Remember, a password is letters, numbers or symbols that keep data safe. You can join the network after you have entered the correct password.

To join a new network, you will need to search for available wi-fi networks. Let's practise how to do this.

Activity 3

Searching for wi-fi networks

> You will need:
> a desktop computer, laptop or tablet with internet access,
> a pencil and paper or a whiteboard pen and mini whiteboard

Find the wi-fi button on your computer. Click or tap on it to see the name of your network.

1. Write down the name of the network you are connected to.
2. What other networks are available on your digital device?
3. Do any of them have padlocks next to them?

127

3 Networks and digital communication

Did you know?

If there is no wi-fi available, a mobile phone can act as a router. It can share its internet connection with another digital device.

You have been learning about problems connecting to the internet.

If you have a problem when you are learning about something, what can you do to fix it? How can you get help?

Look what I can do!

- ☐ I can say which digital devices can connect to a network.
- ☐ I know that there are wired and wireless networks.
- ☐ I can say when a network is and is not available.

> 3.2 Why have a network?

We are going to:

- find out why it can be useful to connect digital devices to a network
- understand that devices in a network share information
- learn about problems that can happen when digital devices connect to a network.

connect   network
digital device   risk
email   virus

Getting started

What do you already know?

- Some digital devices connect to a network with a wired connection.
- Some digital devices connect to a network with a wireless connection.
- Sometimes there are problems connecting to a network.

3 Networks and digital communication

Continued

Now try this!

Here are some things that digital devices can do when they are connected (joined) together. Which ones have you done before?

- Sent a picture to a printer.
- Sent a message to a friend at school who is working in the computer room.
- Made a presentation with a friend on another computer.
- Saved a piece of computing work at school.

Can you think of any other things you can do when digital devices are connected together?

3.2 Why have a network?

Connecting computers

At Arun's school, they connect lots of digital devices to the school network.

Connecting digital devices is more useful than using them on their own. You can share information between them.

Arun is using a computer that is not connected to a network. He saves his work on that computer. Now he must always use the same computer to see his work.

If Arun had used a computer that was connected to a network, he could use any computer on that network to see his work.

3   Networks and digital communication

If we connect two computers together, we can send our work to someone else. We can also look at the same piece of work at the same time.

Sharing information across a network

We have learnt about connecting computers using a small network, like a school network.

We can also connect computers to bigger networks. The biggest network in the world is the internet!

Digital devices can share different types of information when they are connected over the internet.

We can send:

3.2 Why have a network?

Unplugged activity 1

What are they sending?

You will need:
a pencil and paper or a whiteboard pen and mini whiteboard

Write down what type of file each person is sending.

I am sending a song I like to my cousin.

I am sending a written message to my grandma.

I am sending a recording of a dance to my teacher.

Stay safe!

Personal data must not be shared with others online.

This is information that you should keep private, such as your full name, where you live, your date of birth.

Always check with an adult before you share anything online.

3 Networks and digital communication

Different ways of sending

When documents are saved on a computer that is connected to the internet, we can share them with others.

They can be shared using **email** (an electronic way of sending messages) or with a messaging app or program.

The internet lets us share information very quickly with someone who is in another town, city, or even another country.

> **Did you know?**
>
> When digital devices send large amounts of information across a network, the information is split into small pieces. This makes it easier to send.

3.2 Why have a network?

Unplugged activity 2

Why use a network?

> You will need:
> a pencil and paper or a whiteboard pen and mini whiteboard

Sofia has a picture of her new pet.
She wants to send it to Arun.

It is better if I print it out and post it to you.

It is better if you send it to me using an online messaging service.

1. Write down three reasons that Arun might say this.
2. Who do you agree with? Write down your reasons.
3. Have you ever sent a message or picture over a network?

Share your reasons with a partner. Did they think of the same things as you, or different ones?

3 Networks and digital communication

Being careful on a network

You have learnt about connecting digital devices to a small network, like school or home, or a much larger network, like the internet.

You know that it can be useful.

Now you will learn about some of the **risks** of connecting to a network. Risks are things that we have to be careful of. They can be dangerous or make problems.

Information saved on networks needs to be kept safe so that only people who you know and trust can see it.

If we catch a cold, we have a **virus**. Did you know that computers can catch viruses too?

Computers can catch viruses when they connect to unsafe networks. Just like colds, computer viruses can spread easily. They can spread to other computers on the same network.

A virus might damage your computer by slowing it down. It might be able to see your personal data.

3.2 Why have a network?

Unplugged activity 3

Is it dangerous?

> **You will need:**
> a pencil and paper or a whiteboard pen and mini whiteboard

Zara's computer is connected to her school network. She knows that it is important to keep her computer and the network safe.

Which of these things would keep a network safe? Which things might be dangerous?

Copy the table and put the phrases under the correct headings.

- keeping passwords private
- logging off when we finish using a computer
- sharing passwords with other people
- opening documents sent to us by strangers

Keeps a network safe	Could be dangerous to a network

3 Networks and digital communication

You have been learning about how networks can share information.

How does connecting with other people help you to share information?

Who could you connect with to help with your learning?

Look what I can do!

- [ ] I can say why it is useful to connect devices to a network.
- [ ] I know that digital devices in a network share information.
- [ ] I can talk about some of the problems that can happen when digital devices connect to a network.

3.2 Why have a network?

Project

Make a poster of your school network

You will need:
a pencil and paper, coloured pencils

You have learnt why networks are useful.

Remember, a network is where two or more computers are joined together.

Think about all the digital devices on your school network.

Remember, a digital device is something that does a job. There are lots of digital devices in my school, like laptops and tablets.

139

3 Networks and digital communication

> **Continued**
>
> Draw the digital devices that are connected to your school network and label them.
>
> Use one colour for digital devices that connect with a wired connection.
>
> Use another colour for digital devices that connect using a wireless connection.

3.2 Why have a network?

Check your progress

1. What is Marcus describing?

   > This is an important part of a computer network. It is a device that sends data between computer networks.

2. Wi-fi is another name for a wireless connection to a network. **True** / **False**

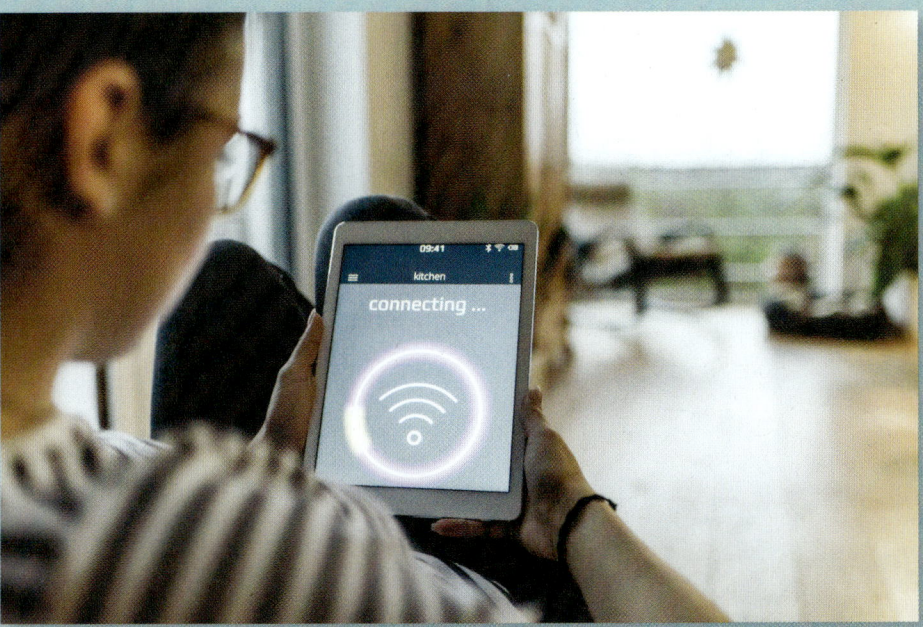

3. Which of these would you need a network connection for?

   A To type up a story

   B To send a message to a friend's computer

   C To make a digital painting

3 Networks and digital communication

Continued

4 Zara is trying to think of digital devices that can be connected to a network at the doctor's surgery.

She has thought of the printer on the desk.

Can you think of two more?

5 Name one useful thing about connecting to a network.

6 Which one of these could be dangerous to a network?

   A Using a computer for a long time

   B Keeping your password private

   C Sharing your computer password with a friend

4 Computer systems

> 4.1 Hardware and software

We are going to:
- find out what hardware is and look at some examples
- learn what input devices are
- learn what output devices are
- understand what software is
- find out how we can use software.

app
computer system
function
hardware
input
input device
output
output device
software
touchscreen

143

4 Computer systems

Getting started

What do you already know?

- There are different types of computers.
- Computers run applications and programs that allow us to do different things.
- There are different ways to input (send in) information to a computer.
- There are different ways that computers can output (send out) information.

Now try this!

What different types of computer can you remember?

Work with a partner. Tell them which types of computers you remember.

Did they remember any types of computers that you did not?

I can remember that a laptop is a type of computer.

4.1 Hardware and software

Hardware

Sometimes we connect (join) extra parts to computers.

Extra parts that we can see or touch are called hardware.

When we connect hardware to a computer, we make a computer system.

A computer system is the name for a computer and all the hardware that is connected to it.

Look at this picture. You are going to look for pieces of hardware.

I can see the screen so that must be hardware.

The boy can touch the mouse, so that must be hardware.

Questions

1. What other examples of hardware can you see in the picture?
2. What was the last piece of hardware you used?

4 Computer systems

Unplugged activity 1

Hardware hunt

> **You will need:**
> a pencil and paper or a whiteboard pen and mini whiteboard

Look around your classroom. Find an example of some hardware that is used with a computer. Draw a picture of it.

Show the picture to a partner.

Can your partner say which piece of hardware you have drawn? Which piece of hardware has your partner drawn?

4.1 Hardware and software

What does hardware do?

Each piece of hardware has its own **function**.
This means that each piece does something different.

I use the mouse to choose things on the computer screen.

The computer uses the speakers to play sounds.

Question

3 Look at this picture.

Which term from the boxes completes each sentence?

a The boy uses the _____ to choose what to watch.

b The _____ shows what the boy has chosen.

147

4 Computer systems

Unplugged activity 2

What is my function?

> **You will need:**
> a pencil and paper or a whiteboard pen and mini whiteboard

You can see some pieces of computer hardware below.

You can also see the function of each piece of computer hardware, but they are mixed up. Match the computer hardware with its function.

Write down the letter that matches each number. I will do the first one for you: 1 = E.

Computer hardware

1 mouse

2 keyboard

3 printer

4 screen

5 speaker

Function

A You use it to enter letters and numbers into the computer.

B It shows you information.

C It plays sounds.

D It makes a paper copy of words or pictures.

E You use it to move around the screen and click on things.

4.1 Hardware and software

> **Continued**
>
> **How am I doing?**
>
> Share your answers with another learner.
> Do you have the same answers?
>
> If your answers are different, decide together which one is right.

You have been learning about the functions of different hardware. Think about the hardware that you use.

Does using it help you understand its function? Would this help you explain its function to someone else?

4 Computer systems

Unplugged activity 3

Hardware diary

> **You will need:**
> a pencil and paper or a whiteboard pen and mini whiteboard

Arun uses lots of different types of hardware with his computer. He wants to know which piece of hardware he uses the most.

He makes a table like the one below.

I am going to add a tick every time I use a piece of hardware.

Copy this table. Over the next week, add a tick each time you use a piece of hardware.

Hardware	Add one tick each time you use it
headphones	
mouse	
keyboard	
printer	

Did you use all of the pieces of hardware?
Which piece of hardware did you use the most?

How am I doing?

Show your hardware diary to a partner. Tell them what you used the piece of hardware for.

I used the keyboard the most. I use the keyboard to type messages to my friends and to write stories.

4.1 Hardware and software

> **Did you know?**
>
> Many countries use a 'QWERTY' keyboard. It is called this because 'QWERTY' are the first six letters on the keyboard.
>
>

Input devices and output devices

Some pieces of hardware are called **input devices**. What do you think these do? We can use what we already know to work it out!

You know that **input** means to put information into the computer.

You know that a device is something that does a task or group of tasks.

So, input devices send information to the computer. Then the computer can use this information.

Some pieces of hardware are called **output devices**.

Remember, **output** means that information comes out of the computer. So output devices share information that has come from the computer.

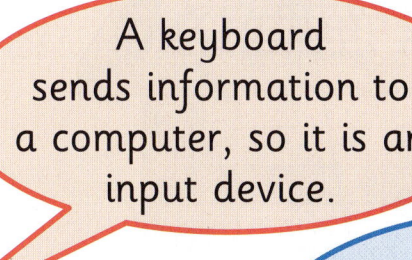

A keyboard sends information to a computer, so it is an input device.

A screen shows me pictures from the computer, so it is an output device.

4 Computer systems

Unplugged activity 4

Input or output devices?

> **You will need:**
> a pencil and paper or a whiteboard pen and mini whiteboard

Copy this table.

Input devices	Output devices

Look at these pieces of hardware. Are they input devices or output devices?

Write the names or draw a picture of the device in the correct part of the table.

Think about whether information goes **in** to the computer (**in**put) or comes **out** of the computer (**out**put).

printer, speaker, screen, mouse, keyboard

4.1 Hardware and software

Inputs and outputs

Sometimes a device is both an input device *and* an output device.

This computer has a **touchscreen**. A touchscreen is a screen that you can touch to send information to the computer.

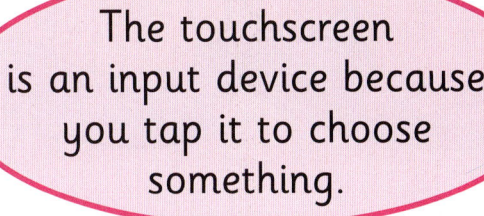
The touchscreen is an input device because you tap it to choose something.

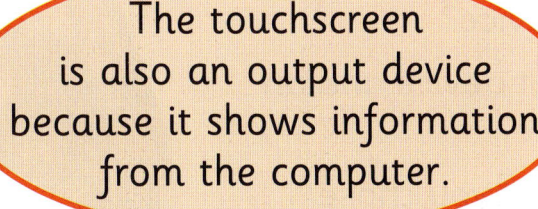
The touchscreen is also an output device because it shows information from the computer.

153

4 Computer systems

Questions

Look at the picture, then answer the questions.

If you press the game controller buttons, a character on the screen moves.

If a character on the screen falls, the game controller vibrates. That means it moves quickly from side to side.

4   Is the controller:

   A   an input device?

   B   an output device?

   C   both an input device and an output device?

5   Tell a partner why you chose your answer to question 3.

154

Software

Remember, extra parts that we can see or touch are called hardware. There are other parts of the computer that you cannot see or touch. These parts are called software.

Computer systems use software to send information to their different parts. Remember, a computer system is the name given to a computer and the hardware connected to it.

When hardware is added to the computer, we use software to send messages between the hardware and different parts of the computer.

I use software when I use my tablet to talk to my friends.

Did you know?

Software is used to help astronauts land on the moon.

4 Computer systems

How do we use software?

You might have learnt about programs and **apps** before. The word app is short for 'software application'.

You will have used software if you used a computer to:

- make a poster
- make some music
- write a story
- make changes to a photo.

We can use apps to make things! My friends use apps on their tablets and apps on their laptops.

4.1 Hardware and software

What does software do?

The type of software that we use depends on what we are going to do. Different types of software have different functions. Remember, function means job.

> I am making a poster about my favourite animals.
> I am using software that lets me add words and pictures.

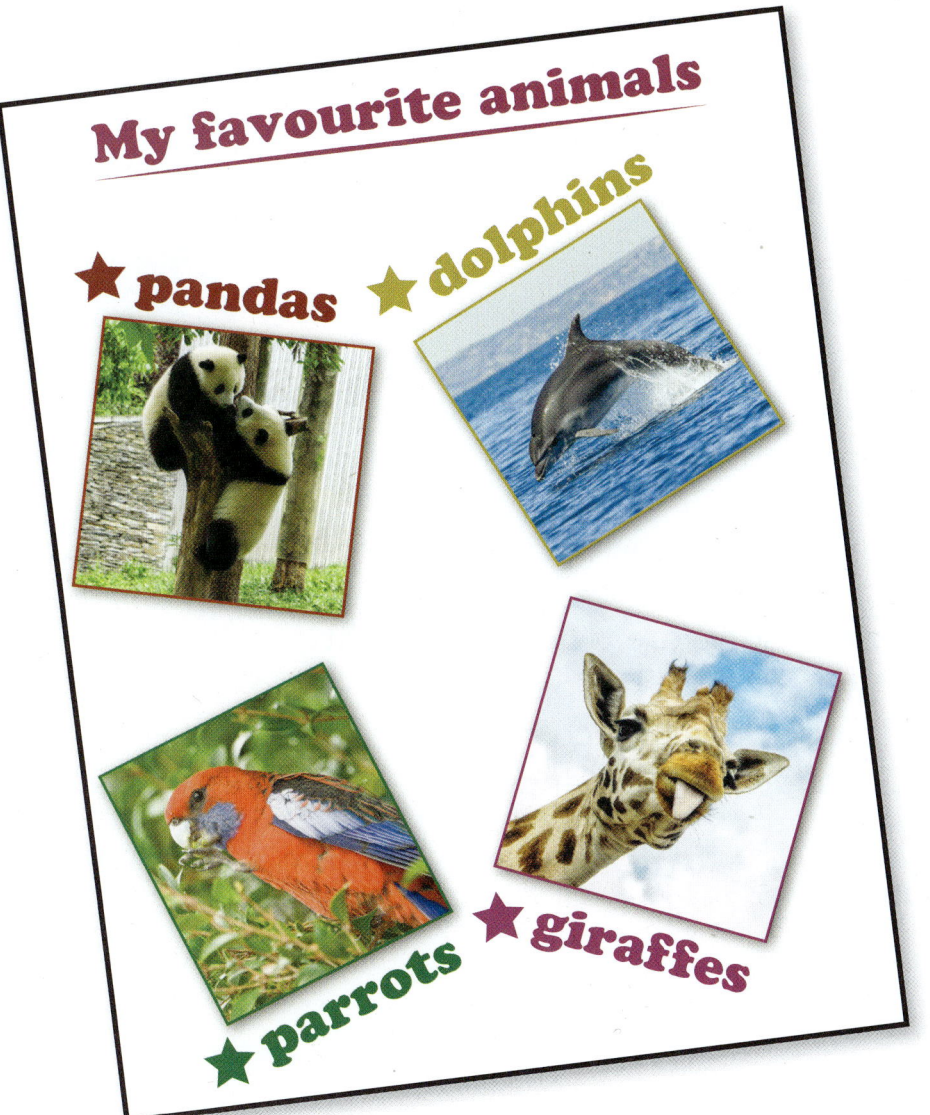

4 Computer systems

Unplugged activity 5

Party invites

I want to make invitations to a party. Which type of software application should I use?

These are the functions of three types of software. Choose which one Sofia should use. Why did you choose it?

1. Adds text, changes text size and style
2. Adds text and images, changes layout
3. Adds video clips, edits video clips, adds sounds, adds text

How am I doing?

Tell a partner which software you chose for Sofia and why you picked it. Did your partner choose the same software?

When we choose which type of software to use, we might pick a different type of software from other people. This because there are different ways to record the information that we want to share with other people. We can share information by:

- typing using a keyboard
- recording our voice
- recording a video.

4.1 Hardware and software

Activity 6

Tell a joke!

> You will need:
> a desktop computer, laptop or tablet

Think of a joke or funny story that has made you laugh.
You are going to use an app to record your joke.
You can use one of these:

- voice recording software
- video recording software
- writing software.

Choose how you would like to record your joke.
You only need to pick one way of recording the joke.
Then choose the best app to do this.

What is the name of the software that you used?

I like this joke: What is an astronaut's favourite key on the keyboard? The space bar!
I will record it using a voice recording app.

4 Computer systems

We have learnt about some different types of software. How do you decide which software you use?

Do you think about the functions of different software when deciding?

Look what I can do!

☐ I know what hardware is and can find examples of hardware.

☐ I can describe the difference between input and output devices.

☐ I know what software is.

☐ I can explain what I have used application software (apps) for.

> 4.2 Different types of computer

We are going to:
- learn about the different ways that some computers are used
- understand how computers are easy to use
- think about why we choose a type of computer.

battery   portable
desktop computer   smartphone
digital camera   smart speaker
laptop   tablet
microphone

Getting started

What do you already know?
- Hardware devices are used with computers.
- Input devices send information to a computer.
- Output devices use information from the computer.

Now try this!

Look at this photo. What computers are being used? Can you name any other types of computer?

Talk to a partner. Tell them the computers you named. Did they name any that you did not?

4 Computer systems

There are lots of different types of computers.
Some computers are used in different ways.

Let's look at the ways some computers are used.

Using tablets

Lots of people like to use **tablet** computers.
These are very small, light computers.

Tablets are just one flat screen – they do not fold.
Here are some reasons why people like tablets:

- They are very easy to use.
- You do not need a keyboard or mouse to use a tablet – you just tap the screen.
- Tablets are **portable**. If something is portable, it is easy to carry around and take to different places.

tablet

To choose something, I tap a picture on the screen.

4.2 Different types of computer

I also tap the screen to use the keyboard. This means that I can write messages to my friends.

Using desktop computers and laptops

Remember, a **desktop computer** is a computer that is difficult to carry around with you.

A **laptop** is easier to carry – the screen can be folded flat against the keyboard.

If you are using a desktop computer or a laptop, you can choose things in a different way. You can use a mouse.

desktop computer with a keyboard and mouse

laptop with a mouse

163

4 Computer systems

A mouse is made to fit in your hand. It is easy to use because it fits the shape of your hand.

Your fingers can comfortably click the buttons. When you move the mouse, the pointer on the screen moves:

There are buttons on the mouse to press when you want to choose something. You press the buttons with your fingers.

You move the pointer to the thing you want to choose. Then you click a button to choose it.

Most laptop computers have a touchpad. This allows you to move the pointer around the screen and click on what you want to choose without using a mouse. To use a touchpad, you move your finger across it. The pointer follows the movement you make with your finger. To select something you press the touchpad.

Question

1 Think back to what you learnt in Topic 4.1. Is a mouse an input device or an output device? Remember, a mouse sends information to the computer.

If you want to type text into a desktop computer, you need to add a keyboard. To type, you press the key which contains the letter you want to use. Keyboards are designed to be used by both of your hands. Laptops also use a keyboard, but this is part of the laptop. Some people can type using all of their fingers and without looking at the keys. This is called touch typing.

> **Stay safe!**
>
> We need to take care if we are connecting (joining) a keyboard or a mouse to our computer. If we try to connect them in the wrong place, we can damage the computer.

4.2 Different types of computer

> **Did you know?**
>
> Some video game controllers can have 16 different buttons to press.
>
> You can press any of these buttons using your fingers or thumbs.
>
> All of the buttons are in places that you can reach easily with your fingers.

Digital cameras

Remember, a digital device is something that contains a computer and can do a task (job) or group of tasks.

When digital devices are designed, people think about how to make them easy to use.

Sofia is using a **digital camera** to take a photo of some trees. A digital camera takes photos and stores (keeps) them.

digital camera

A digital camera has a small screen that shows us the photo we have taken.

This means we can check whether the photo we took is good enough to keep.

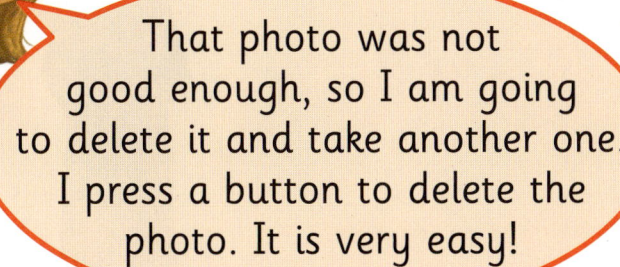

That photo was not good enough, so I am going to delete it and take another one. I press a button to delete the photo. It is very easy!

165

4 Computer systems

Smart speakers

We can use some digital devices by talking to them. These digital devices are called **smart speakers** or digital assistants.

Have you used a smart speaker?

What did you say to it? How did it answer you?

Smart speakers answer our questions and follow simple instructions.

They are easy to use because we can control them just by talking to them, like we would talk to another human.

We do not even need to touch them. This is useful when we have things in our hands.

We can ask the smart speaker questions.

smart speaker

What time is it?

What will the weather be like today?

4.2 Different types of computer

We can also give the smart speaker instructions.

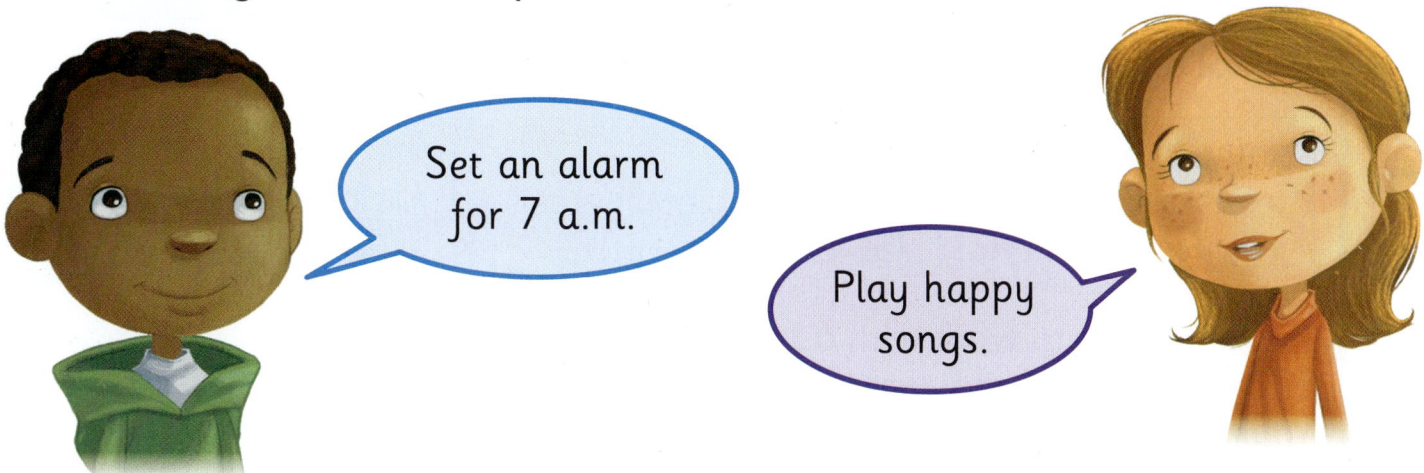

Set an alarm for 7 a.m.

Play happy songs.

Smart speakers talk back to us to answer our questions. They also tell us when they have followed an instruction.

Marcus is doing some baking. He is using a smart speaker to help him.

Should I use plain flour or self-raising flour?

You should use 150 grams of plain flour.

4 Computer systems

Activity 1

Digital device poster

> **You will need:**
> a desktop computer, laptop or tablet, source files
> **4.1_poster_template** and **4.2_device_pictures**

You are going to work with a partner to make a poster about a digital device and how it is used. Your teacher will give you a poster template to work with.

Choose one of the digital devices you have been learning about.

Write the name of the digital device as the title of your poster.

Use the folder of pictures your teacher will give you. Add a picture of your device to the poster.

Complete the sentences on the poster to describe your digital device.

> This is a _____.
> To use it, you need to _____.

> Draw a picture of a person next to the digital device. Draw an arrow to the part of their body that they use to control the digital device.

4.2 Different types of computer

Which computer should I use?

Sometimes we choose a computer because of the job we are doing. If we need to see something in lots of detail, we need a big screen.

These people are planning how to make an engine. They are using desktop computers with screens.

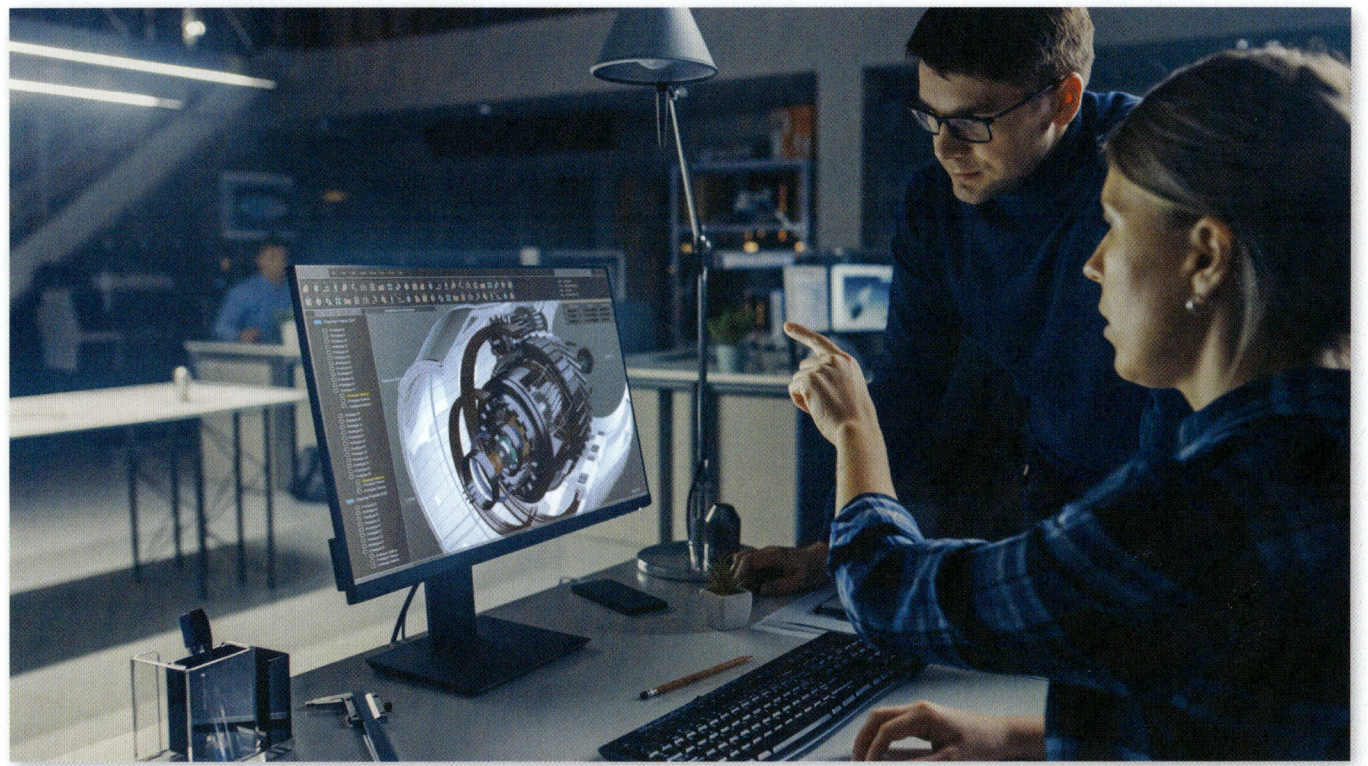

Wow! The screen makes the pictures easier to see.

169

4 Computer systems

If we need to take a photo, we need something that is small and light so we can hold it up easily.

Smartphones are like small computers. They have cameras and it is easy to take photos on them.

Sometimes we choose a computer because of where we are.

Laptops are smaller and lighter than desktop computers.

They are portable. Remember, this means they can be easily moved from one place to another.

Tablets and smartphones are even smaller and lighter than laptops!

I took my laptop when I visited my grandma. I packed it in my bag.

I took my tablet to the theme park. It was not too heavy to carry around all day.

Stay safe!

If you are using a portable computer, make sure you put it away safely when you finish using it. Every year, 70 million smartphones are lost in the USA!

4.2 Different types of computer

Unplugged activity 2

Which computer?

You will need:
a pencil and paper or a whiteboard pen and mini whiteboard

Look at these three examples.

Which type of computer do you think should be used for each activity? Explain why you chose each type of computer.

smartphone   desktop computer   tablet

1. Sofia is inside the house. She wants to type a letter to her cousin.

2. Marcus is in the garden. He wants to know the names of some flowers.

171

4 Computer systems

> **Continued**

3   Zara is on a long train journey to see her relatives. She wants to play games.

How am I doing?

Talk about your answers with a partner.

They might have different answers from you. That does not mean they are wrong.

Some questions may have more than one answer. Explain the reasons why you chose each computer.

Question

2   Think of another activity someone might do using a desktop computer, tablet or smartphone. Which type of computer would they use?

Tell your partner the activity and ask them which computer they would use. Did they pick the same computer as you?

4.2 Different types of computer

What do I want the computer to do?

Sometimes we choose a computer because of what we want it to do.

Sofia likes playing video games. She plays her games on a games console.

Games consoles can show clear pictures. The games might be very detailed, with lots of levels and characters.

Sofia can save her game on the games console and come back to it later.

> **Did you know?**
>
> The same video game will be different on a games console and a tablet or smartphone.
>
> A game on a tablet or smartphone is often called the 'mobile version' to show that it is not exactly the same as the one on the games console.
>
>

4 Computer systems

Batteries

Laptops, smartphones and tablets all have a **battery**. The battery gives these digital devices power when they are not plugged in.

This means the devices can be used in different places. When the battery runs out, the computer will need to be plugged into a charger.

This charges the battery, which means it gives the battery power again.

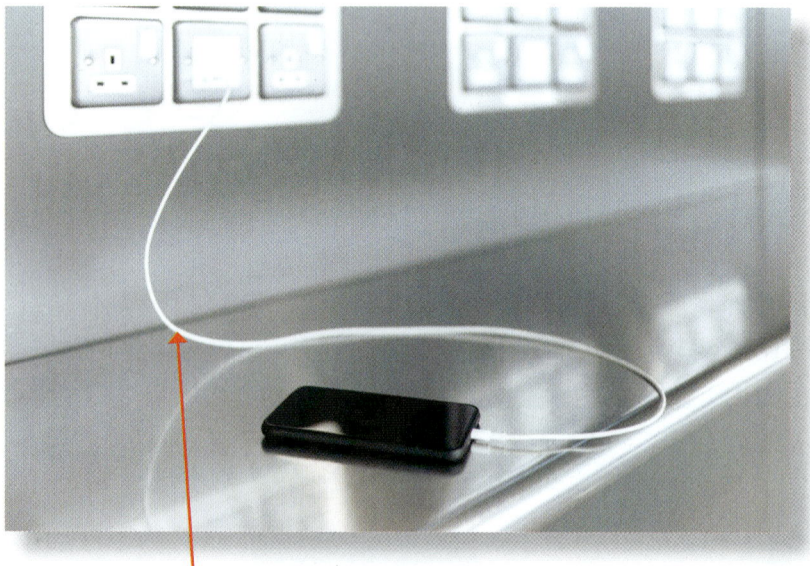

This smartphone is having its battery charged

The batteries in smartphones and tablets last longer than the ones in laptops.

Smartphones and tablets are useful if you will be out all day with nowhere to charge them.

174

4.2 Different types of computer

Unplugged activity 3

Computer matching

> You will need:
> a pencil and paper or a whiteboard pen and mini whiteboard

Match each type of computer to what the children are describing. Write down your answers.

1.

2.

3.

Ⓐ This computer uses a battery. The battery might not last very long.

Ⓑ This computer needs to be plugged in to be used.

Ⓒ This computer uses a battery. The battery should last a long time.

175

4 Computer systems

It is useful to know what different computers can and cannot do well. This allows you to select the right computer to use for the task you are doing.

Unplugged activity 4

Video calling

Zara wants to video call her family members who live in another country. She is deciding which of her computers to use.

She wants her family to see and hear her. She also wants to be able to see and hear her family.

The table below has information about the types of computer that Zara has.

Look at the table. What type of computer should Zara use?

Zara's computers	Does it have a microphone?	Does it have a camera?	Does it have speakers?	Does it have a screen?
desktop computer	yes	no	yes	yes (large)
laptop	yes	yes	yes	yes (medium)
smartphone	yes	yes	yes	yes (small)

A **microphone** is something that records and sends sounds.

4.2 Different types of computer

> **Continued**
>
> **How am I doing?**
>
> Did you think about how Zara would see and hear her family using the computer?
>
> Did you think about how Zara's family would be able to see and hear her?
>
> Tell a partner which computer you chose, and why.

Look what I can do!

- ☐ I know the different ways that some computers are used.
- ☐ I understand how computers are easy to use.
- ☐ I can explain the reasons why we might choose a computer.

177

4 Computer systems

> 4.3 Computers, humans and robots

We are going to:
- learn about how robots are made to do certain jobs
- learn about the jobs that computers can do better than humans
- find out which things are the same in most robots
- learn how real-life robots are different to robots in fiction.

> calculator
> input
> robot

Getting started

What do you already know?
- People use software to make things.
- A digital device has a computer and does a task or a number of tasks.
- Lots of digital devices are controlled by computers.
- Robots are digital devices that can do jobs without much help from humans.
- Some robots are used to help people.

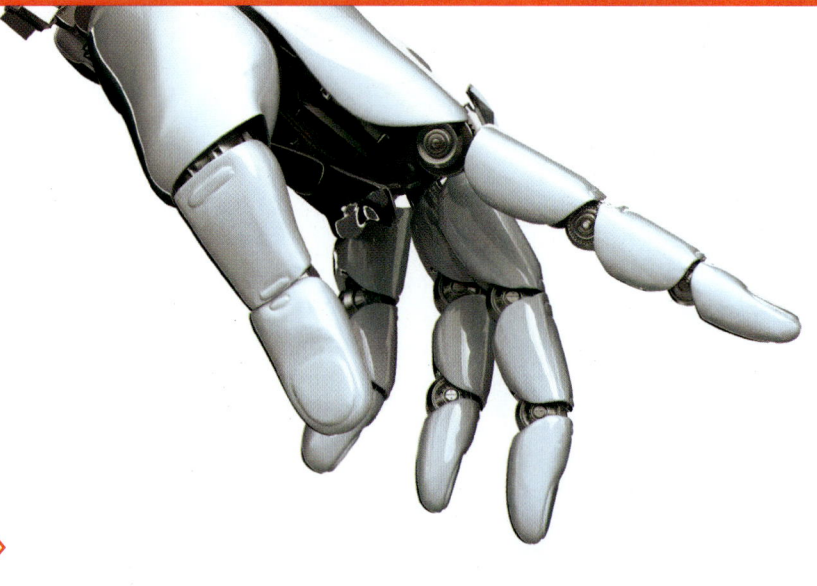
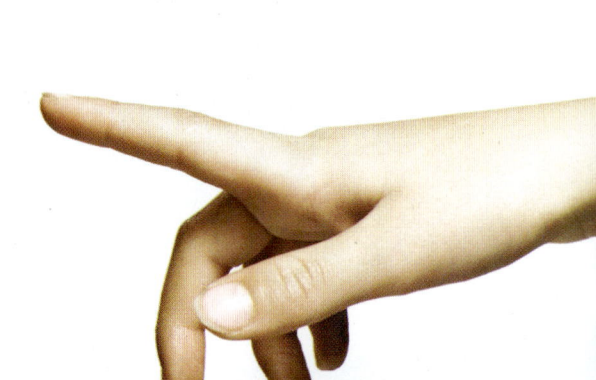

4.3 Computers, humans and robots

Continued

Now try this!

Look at these photos of some digital devices. They have different parts that work together to do a job and use power to move their parts.

Device 1

Device 2

Work with a partner. Can you name any differences between the two devices? Think about:

- what they look like
- the jobs that they do
- whether you might see them in your home.

4 Computer systems

Using computers to help us

Computers can do some tasks (jobs) instead of humans. This is because they are better at doing the tasks than humans.

This person is using a **calculator**. A calculator is a type of digital device and contains a computer.

Calculators can work out calculations for us. They give the correct answer every time.

When we are tired, we can make mistakes.

Calculators do not get tired.

Some houses use digital devices to control their air conditioning.

The computer in the digital device keeps checking the temperature in the house. If it is too hot, it turns the air conditioning on. When it is cool enough, it turns the air conditioning off.

A computer can keep checking the temperature and making changes. This saves people time.

4.3 Computers, humans and robots

Computers can be used to control digital devices. This device has been given instructions to pick up small pieces of metal.

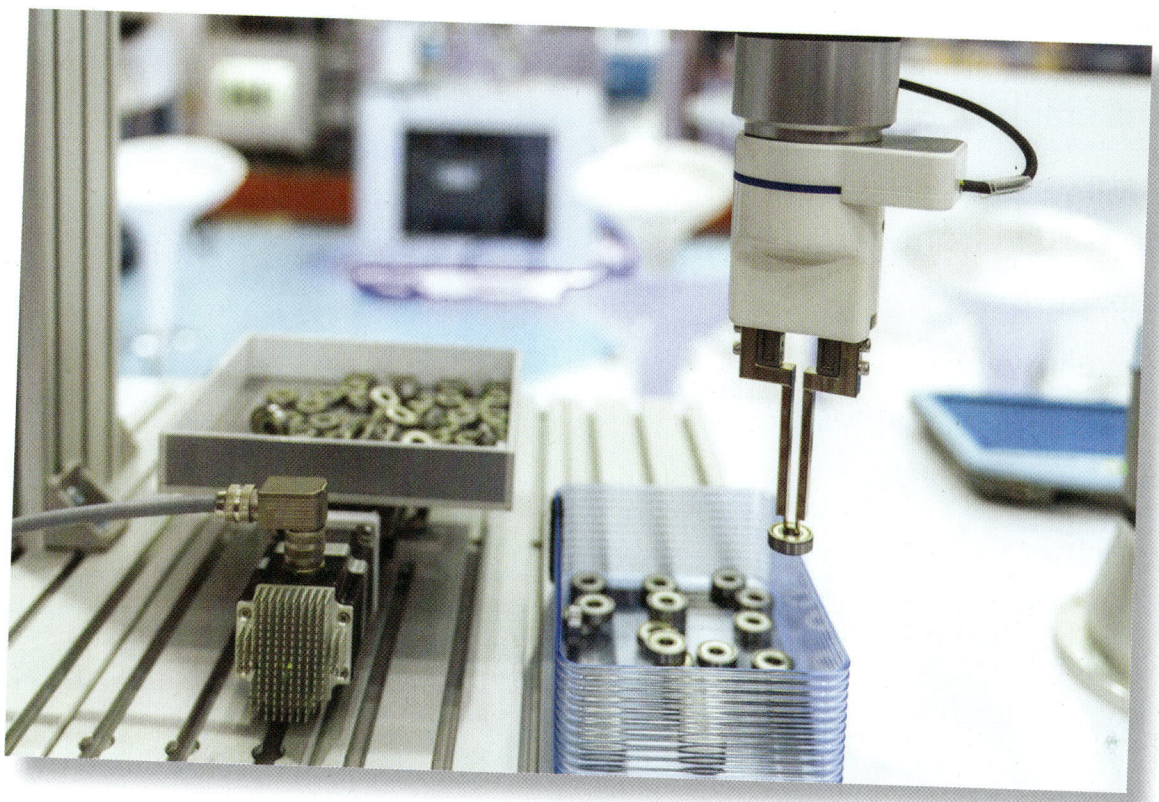

Here are four reasons why a digital device does this job instead of a human:

- The device does not get tired.
- The device does not need to take a break.
- The device does not get bored with doing the same job lots of times.
- The device is faster.

Work with a partner. Which do you think is the best reason for using a digital device instead of a human?

Join another pair. Explain to them why you have picked your reason.

4 Computer systems

Unplugged activity 1

Could you do a computer's job?

> **You will need:**
> coloured pencils, small pieces of card, three pots (like clean, empty yoghurt pots), a pen

Write the following words on the three pieces of card. Place each card in front of one of the pots:

- red, blue, purple
- orange, yellow, brown
- green, pink, black.

Work with a partner.

Ask your partner to count to ten.
At the same time, you have to sort the coloured pencils into the correct pot.

How quickly can you do it? Now swap so you count and your partner sorts the pencils.

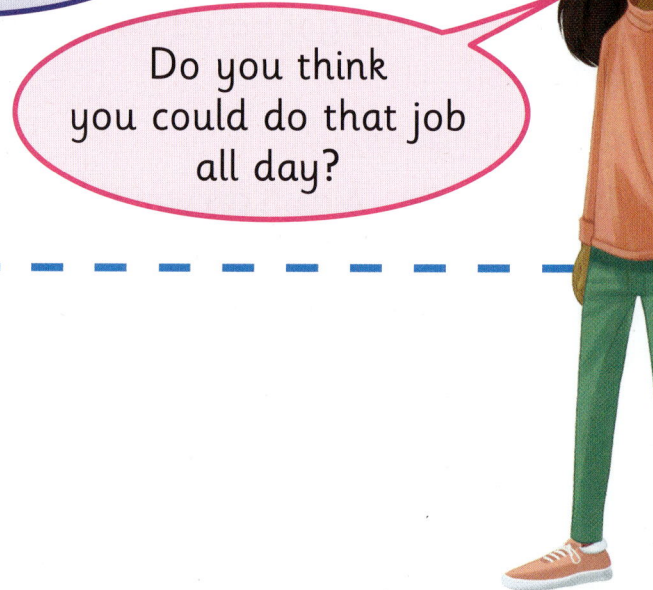

How many pencils did you sort? Did you make any mistakes?

Do you think you could do that job all day?

4.3 Computers, humans and robots

> **Did you know?**
>
> Robots are used in space. They fix satellites that are going around the Earth.

You have done the sort of job that a computer in a digital device might do.

Now do you understand why computers are better at doing some jobs than humans?

Does this mean computers do every job better than humans?

4 Computer systems

What do humans do better than a computer?

There are lots of jobs that humans are better at doing than computers.

Humans are better than computers at jobs that involve looking after people. A computer would not be able to care for someone in a hospital.

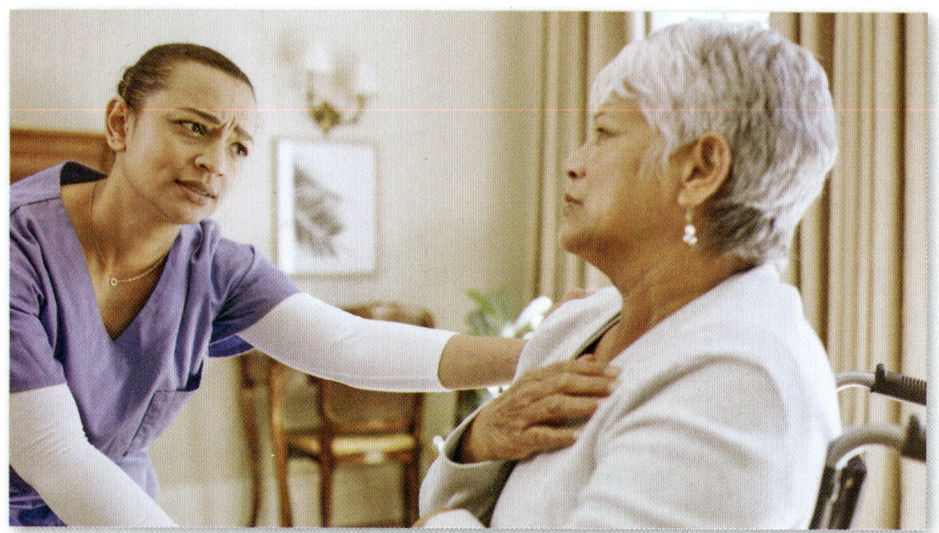

Humans are better than computers at jobs where new and creative ideas are needed. Humans are good at coming up with new and different ways of doing things. They are also good at listening to other people and working together.

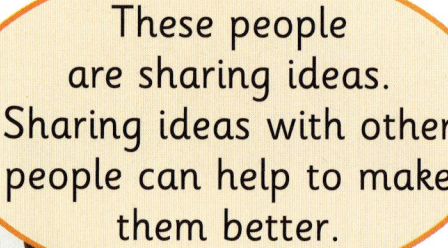

These people are sharing ideas. Sharing ideas with other people can help to make them better.

4.3 Computers, humans and robots

Unplugged activity 2

A computer or human job?

> **You will need:**
> a pencil and paper or a whiteboard pen and mini whiteboard

You will work in a group for this activity. Draw a table like the one below.

Job for a computer	Job for a human

Humans are better at jobs which involve listening to people's feelings and making decisions. A computer cannot tell the difference between right and wrong.

Look at the jobs below. Decide for each one if a computer or a human would be better at it. Add it to the correct part of your table.

- sorting tinned food
- adding up the price of shopping
- looking after someone who is unwell
- helping someone who is upset
- lifting heavy objects all day long
- teaching someone to swim

How are we doing?

Pick one job that a computer does better than a human.

Why does a computer do this job better than a human? Explain to your group.

The group should say whether your explanation makes sense.

4 Computer systems

Robot fact or robot fiction?

Robots are devices that do jobs without much help from humans.

I am going to dress up as a robot.

Are you going to dress up as a robot from a story or a real-life robot?

Most robots that we see in fiction (in books or in films) look a bit like humans.

This robot has a face, a body, arms and legs, just like most humans. In stories, robots often act like humans too.

Sometimes robots have feelings. This robot looks very sad.

186

4.3 Computers, humans and robots

Real-life robots

Some people think robots have to look and act like humans.
In the real world, robots do not have to look like humans.
Robots do not have feelings.

There are some things that robots usually do:

- Robots collect information.
- Robots use the information they have collected.
  This helps robots know when they need to do their job.
- Robots move. Moving means that robots can do their jobs.

Robots are made with everything they need to do their job. What they look like will depend on the job they have to do.

This robot is making cars. Its job is to make cars.
The robot does not feel happy when it has made a car.

4 Computer systems

Question

This robot is used to move boxes from one place to another. It follows the yellow line to move between places.

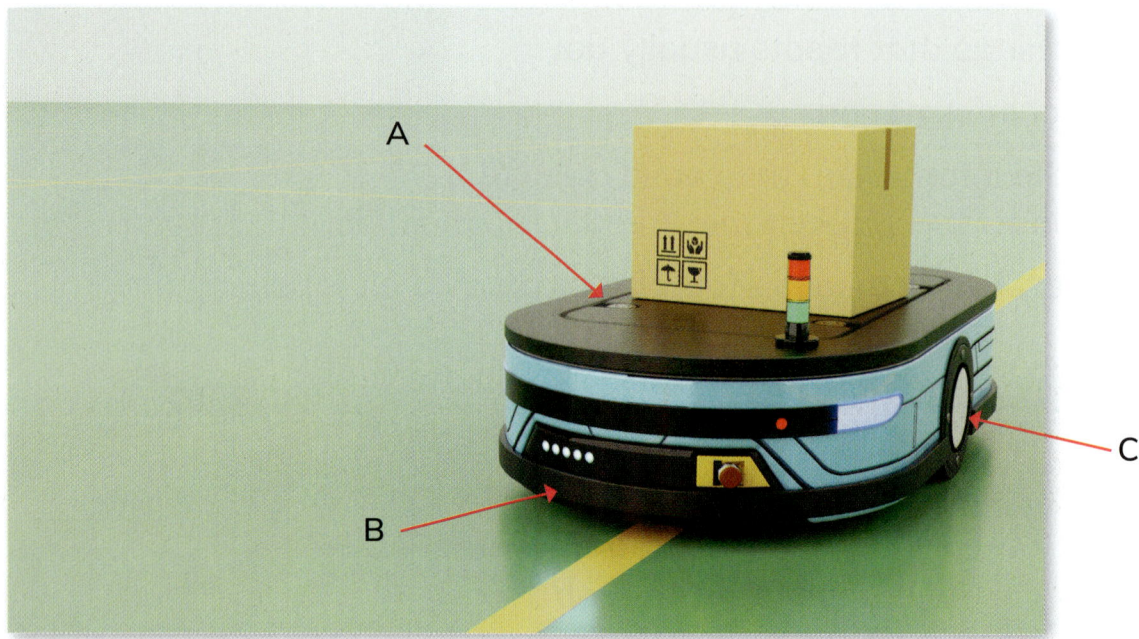

Work with a partner. Look at the sentences below.

Match each sentence with the correct label (A–C) in the picture above to describe how the robot does its job. Write down your answers.

1 This collects information so that the robot can follow the yellow line.

2 These move the robot.

3 This collects information to check whether there is a box on top.

4.3 Computers, humans and robots

Unplugged activity 3

Car wash

> You will need:
> a pencil and paper or a whiteboard pen and mini whiteboard

A car wash is a type of robot. Which photo is a real-world robot car wash?

When it is doing its job, a car wash does three things:
- it collects information
- it uses the information
- it moves.

Look at the three steps below. They describe how the car wash does its job. Put them in the correct order.

1. The car wash moves the brushes to clean the car.
2. The car wash collects information about how far away the car is.
3. The car wash uses the information to know when to move the brushes.

4 Computer systems

Unplugged activity 4

Sofia's poster

"I have made a poster to show the difference between robots in fiction and real-life robots."

4.3 Computers, humans and robots

Continued

Make a robot poster

> You will need:
> pencils and paper, glue

Work with a partner. Make a poster like Sofia's by drawing a picture of a robot in fiction and a robot in real life.

Then copy the following sentences to the correct part of the poster.

- Robots look a bit like humans.
- Robots do not look like humans. They are made with everything they need to do their job.
- Robots act like humans.
- Robots act the way they need to act to do their job.
- Robots have feelings.
- Robots do not have feelings.

191

4 Computer systems

Look what I can do!

- ☐ I know that robots are made to do certain jobs.
- ☐ I know which jobs might be better done by a computer.
- ☐ I know which things are the same in most robots.
- ☐ I know how real-life robots are different to robots in fiction.

Project

Robotic school helper

> You will need:
> a pencil and paper, colouring pencils, (optional: materials to make a model of a robot, e.g. old cereal boxes, coloured foil, glue)

You are going to draw or make a model of a robot to do a certain job in your school. You should think about the job the robot will do.

"My robot is going to sharpen pencils."

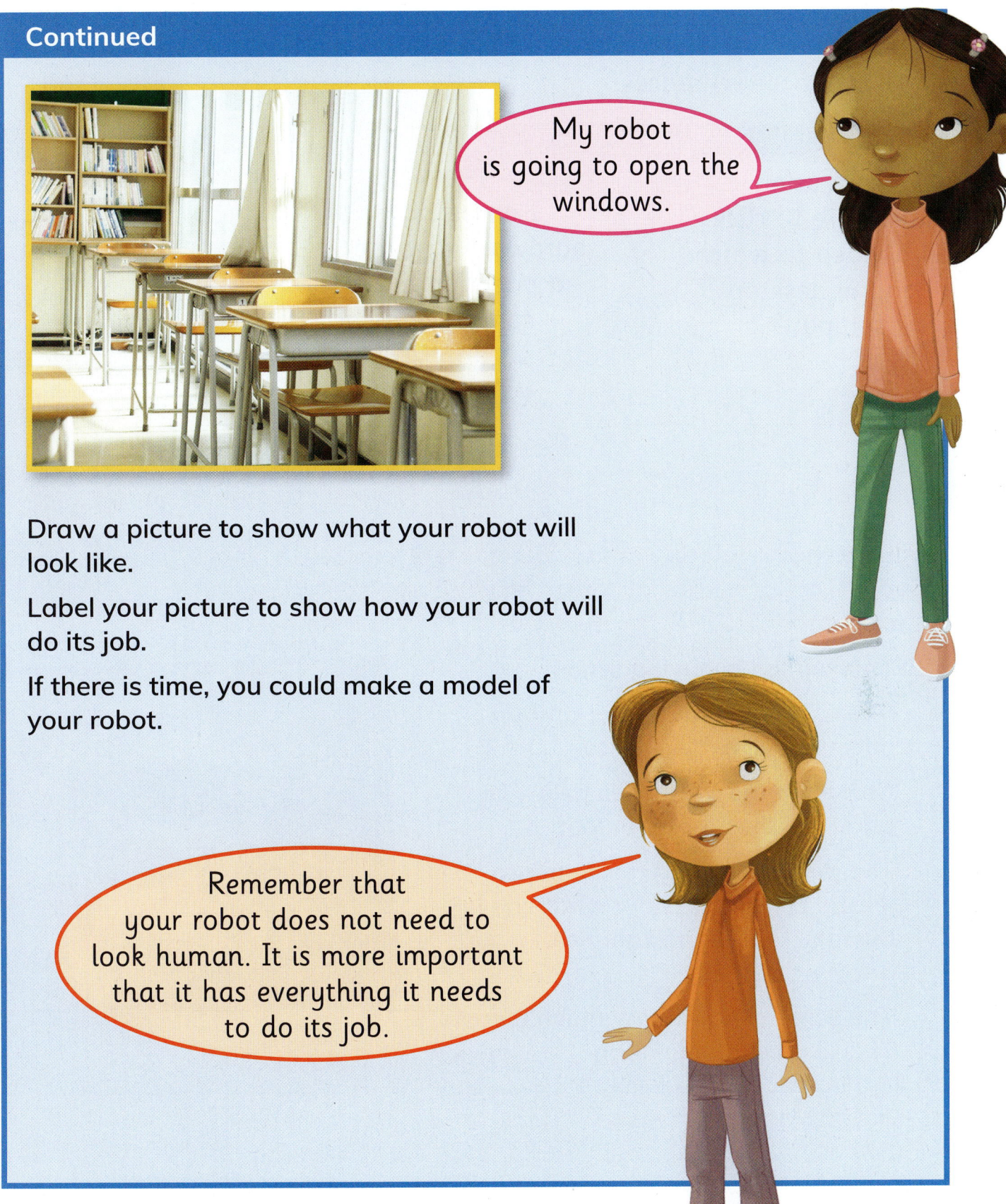

4   Computer systems

Check your progress

1. Read these sentences.

   Which piece of hardware is each character talking about?

   I am using hardware to click on a video to watch on my desktop computer.

   I am using hardware to write a poem on my computer.

   I am using hardware to make a paper copy of a photo I took.

2. This person is buying food.

   She uses an input device and an output device.

   Complete the sentences below by adding either 'input' or 'output'.

   The person is using a scanner to let the computer know what she is buying. This is an example of an _____ device.

   The screen shows how much it costs. This is an example of an _____ device.

Continued

3 Different types of computers are used in different ways.

Match the type of computer with the description of how information is input into the computer.

Type of computer

1 Tablet

2 Desktop computer

3 Video game console

4 Smart speaker

How to input information

A You ask a question or tell it to do something.

B You press a button on the controller.

C You tap the screen to choose something.

D You type on a keyboard.

4 Computer systems

Continued

4 Why has a computer been used for each of these jobs instead of a human?

This robot is moving washing machines.

This computer is checking that nobody is inside the house while the family is away.

Glossary

algorithm	a precise set of instructions	11
	Zara followed the algorithm to build the model.	
animation	a moving image created by a computer	44
	Sofia made a program to create a snake and frog animation.	
app	a computer program that does certain tasks	156
	The app on my brother's smartphone lets him play word games.	
available	something that is ready to be used	126
	The school network was available on Sofia's computer.	
battery	a power source for portable digital devices so they can be used even when they are not plugged in	174
	Zara charged the battery in her tablet.	
block graph	a picture that shows data as blocks	104
	Sofia made a block graph to show how her friends travelled to school.	
bug	an error in a program or algorithm	22
	The bug in the Bee-Bot program made the Bee-Bot go the wrong way.	
calculator	a type of computer that does calculations	180
	Arun used the calculator to add up a list of numbers.	

code	instructions written in a special language that a computer program can understand	45
	Marcus checked that the code he had programmed was correct.	
collect	to gather	88
	We collect data by asking questions.	
command	an instruction that tells a computer what to do	27
	Sofia used the X command to clear the Bee-Bot's memory.	
computer system	a computer and all the hardware that is connected to it	145
	The school bought a new computer system for the classroom.	
connect	to join with something else	117
	Arun is going to connect his computer to a printer.	
data	a piece of data is a fact – it can be a word, number or picture	79
	Zara puts data in the table.	
debug	to look for and correct errors in an algorithm or computer program	22
	We will debug our program because it isn't working properly.	
desktop computer	a computer that you cannot easily carry with you	163
	There is a desktop computer on the table.	
digital camera	a type of camera that can store the photos it takes	165
	Marcus used his mother's digital camera to take a photo of his cat.	

digital device	a piece of equipment that uses a computer to perform a task or a group of tasks	117
	A smartphone is a very useful digital device.	
directions	instructions to make something move	11
	Arun gave his friend directions to his house.	
email	an electronic way of sending messages	134
	Zara set an email to her grandmother while she was on holiday.	
error	something that is not correct; a mistake	22
	I corrected the error in my work.	
form	a list of questions for people to answer used to collect data	86
	I filled out the form online.	
function	the useful thing that something does	147
	The function of a mouse is to choose things on a computer screen.	
graph	a picture that shows data using lines, shapes or colours	103
	I made a graph showing how many pets people in my class have.	
hardware	extra parts added to a computer that make a computer system	145
	A mouse is a piece of hardware.	
input	to send information into a digital device	151
	Arun used the keyboard to input his password.	
input device	a piece of hardware that sends information to a computer	151
	A mouse is an input device. When I move it, information is sent to the computer.	

instructions	a set of words or pictures that tell you what to do or how to make something work *Sofia checked the instructions to find out how to play the game.*	23
laptop	a computer that you can carry; it is flat when you close it *Sofia's mother takes a laptop to work with her.*	163
microphone	a device that records sounds so that they can be used by a computer *Sofia used the microphone to record a song for her friend.*	176
motion	when something moves *The 'Motion commands' make the sprites move.*	47
network	two or more computers that are joined together *My computer, tablet and smartphone are all part of the same network.*	117
network cable	the type of wire used to connect computers to the internet *Arun's computer has a network cable so he can connect to the internet.*	120
non-statistical question	a type of question that can have only one answer *"What is your favourite animal, Marcus?" is a non-statistical question.*	93
organise	to put things in an order that makes sense *Computers can help us to organise data.*	79
output	when a digital device sends out information *The speakers output the video's sound.*	151

output device	a piece of hardware that shares information that comes out of a computer *A computer screen is a type of output device.*	151
password	a set of letters, numbers or symbols that keep data safe *Zara typed in the password to join the school network.*	85
personal data	information about yourself, like your name, age, and where you live *You should never share personal data with people you do not know.*	85
pictogram	a graph that shows data using pictures *Marcus made a pictogram to show what his friends' favourite fruits are.*	106
portable	something that it is easy to carry around *A laptop is a portable device.*	162
precise	includes exact information *Sophia's precise algorithm helped Arun to find her house easily.*	12
predict	to think about what will happen *I predict that the Bee-Bot will turn right.*	28
present	to show something to someone *Marcus used his computer to present his project.*	103
program (noun)	a list of instructions that makes a computer do a task *You can use this program to make a drawing.*	27
program (verb)	putting a list of instructions into a computer to make it do a task *Sofia wants to program the Bee-Bot to move forward.*	31

programming language — the language a computer understands to follow instructions — 45
ScratchJr is a programming language.

record — a collection of data — 81
There is a record on the doctor's computer for Sofia.

repeat — to do something over and over again — 63
Arun made the sprite repeat moving from left to right.

repeat command — a command which instructs the computer to repeat other commands — 63
Zara added a repeat command to her program.

risk — things that we need to be careful of — 136
Marcus knew there was a risk of connecting to a stranger's network.

robot — a device that does jobs without lots of help from humans — 186
The farm uses a robot to look for weeds.

router — a device that manages how data moves between computer networks — 120
The teacher's computer used a router to connect to the internet.

run — if you run the code, you tell the computer to carry out the instructions you have given it — 27
Zara programmed the Bee-Bot and then pressed GO to run her code.

ScratchJr — a programming language — 45
Marcus made a program in ScratchJr.

settings	ways for us to choose how to make a device work	126
	Sofia's father changed the settings on Sofia's tablet to make it safe for her to use.	
smartphone	phones that can be carried around and used like a computer	170
	Zara's sister has a smartphone so she can message her friends.	
smart speaker	a type of digital device that can answer questions and follow simple instructions	166
	Sofia asked the smart speaker what the capital of New Zealand is.	
software	the part of a computer that sends messages between the hardware and different parts of the computer	155
	Software is what we use to talk to someone else on a tablet.	
sprite	the object or character a program controls	46
	Zara added a cat sprite to her program.	
statistical question	a type of question that we need to collect data for in order to answer	93
	"How many of my friends have pets?" is a statistical question.	
store	to keep something so it can be used later	81
	Marcus wants to store data on his tablet.	
tablet	a small, very portable computer	162
	Arun watches videos on his tablet.	
test	to check whether something is correct	14
	We need to test our algorithm to see if it works.	

touchscreen a computer screen that also acts as an input device 153
Sofia used the touchscreen to zoom in on the photo.

trigger a type of command in ScratchJr that starts a program 47
Sofia added a 'Trigger command', which ran the program when she touched the green flag.

virus a program that can damage computers 136
Arun didn't want to open the message in case it contained a virus.

wi-fi a way to connect computers without wires 122
Sofia and Arun use wi-fi to share information between their computers.

wired connection when a computer needs a wire to connect to a network 120
The school computers have a wired connection to the network.

wireless connection when a computer does not need a wire to connect to a network 121
This tablet has a wireless connection to the network.

Acknowledgements

The authors and publishers acknowledge the following sources of copyright material and are grateful for the permissions granted. While every effort has been made, it has not always been possible to identify the sources of all the material used, or to trace all copyright holders. If any omissions are brought to our notice, we will be happy to include the appropriate acknowledgements on reprinting.

Thanks to the following for permission to reproduce images:

Unit 1 Jlbarranco/GI; Pchristinaq/GI; Liam Norris/GI; Brent Hofacker/GI; Ingus Kruklitis/GI; Fatcamera/GI; Peter Dazeley/GI; Pelicankate/GI; Richard Newstead/GI; Bettmann/GI; Peter Cade/GI; Stockplanets/GI; Ghislain & Marie David De Lossy/GI(X2); Stockbyte/GI; Chris Winsor/GI; Peter Atkinson/GI; Gustiawardi Gustiawardi/GI; Peopleimages/GI; Kuritafsheen/GI; Jonathan Kitchen/GI; mladin61/GI; Erik Isakson/GI; Alvarez/GI;
Unit 2 Alexander Spatari/GI; Stockplanets/GI; Martinrlee/GI; David Franklin/GI; Image Source/GI; Fancy/Veer/Corbis/GI; Guido Mieth/GI; Kristina Strasunske/GI; Rick Gayle/GI; Filo/GI; Epoxydude/GI; Tang Ming Tung/GI; Mu_Mu_/GI; Yevgen Romanenko/GI; Juanmonino/GI; Manuel Breva Colmeiro/GI; Andriy Onufriyenko/GI; Paul Bradbury/GI; Tang Ming Tung/GI; Anna Kraynova/GI; JGI/Jamie Grill/GI; Recep-Bg/GI; M-Production/GI; Sally Anscombe/GI; Jose Luis Pelaez Inc/GI; Matthias Kulka/GI; Pixelbay/GI; Ttsz/GI; Fatcamera/GI(X2); Jakeolimb/GI; Klaus Vedfelt/GI; **Unit 2 Source files** Pepifoto/GI; Martinrlee/GI; Hannahargyle/GI; Pornpawit Phosawang/GI; David Franklin/GI; Stockbyte/GI; **Unit 3** Adrienne Bresnahan/GI; Shapecharge/GI; Catherine Delahaye/GI; Andersen Ross Photography Inc/GI; Setthaphat Dodchai/GI; Andrey Bryzgalov/GI; Scanrail/GI; Greg99/GI; Alexsl/GI; Daboost/GI; Adventtr/GI; Kenneth-Cheung/GI; Gary John Norman/GI; Siegfried Layda/GI; Ng Hock How/GI; Carol Yepes/GI; Compassionate Eye Foundation/Chris Ryan/GI; Yuichiro Chino/GI; Marko Geber/GI; Westend61/GI(X2);
Unit 4 Skynesher/GI; Moodboard/GI; Rouzes/GI; Anthony Boulton/GI; Rasslava/GI; Kieran Stone/GI; Amnachphoto/GI; Jamie Grill/GI; Youst/GI; D3sign/GI; Yevgen Romanenko/GI; Encyclopaedia Britannica/GI; VCG/GI; Alexis Rosenfeld/GI; Auscape/GI; Marc Rauw/GI; Mollyanne/GI; Fernando Trabanco Fotografía/GI; Jamie Grill/GI; Lvcandy/GI; ET-Artworks/GI; sweetym/GI; Wat'jna Racha/EyeEm/GI; Jed Share/Kaoru Share/GI; Tetra Images/GI(X2); Olemedia/GI; Gorodenkoff/GI; Marko Geber/GI; Sellwell/GI; Travelcouples/GI; Jeffrey Coolidge/GI; Believe_In_Me/GI; Ariel Skelley/GI; Jamie Grill/GI; Coneyl Jay/GI; Werayuth Tessrimuang/GI; Onurdongel/GI; Eleonora Galli/GI; Alex Tihonov/GI; Prasit Photo/GI; Gerard Mcauliffe/GI; Koto_Feja/GI; Alexanderford/GI; Weekend Images Inc./GI; Westend61/GI; Piranka/GI; Monty Rakusen/GI; Thamrongpat Theerathammakorn/GI; Adelevin/GI; Andy Sotiriou/GI; Ctrphotos/GI; Jpgfactory/GI; Sompong Sriphet/GI; Cravetiger/GI; Nenov/GI; Fatcamera/GI; Japatino/GI; Milatas/GI; Fatcamera/GI; Nicoelnino/GI; Tetra Images/GI; Kate Hiscock/GI; Michael Wapp/GI; Vm/GI; Jozef Polc/GI; Thamrongpat Theerathammakorn/GI

Key GI= Getty Images

Cover illustration by Pablo Gallego (Beehive Illustration)

Bee-Bot is a registered trademark of RM Resources. Illustrations depicting Bee-Bots are created with permission of RM Resources.

Minecraft is a trademark of the Microsoft group of companies. Screenshot of Minecraft used with permission from Microsoft.

Scratch is a project of the Scratch Foundation, in collaboration with the Lifelong Kindergarten Group at the MIT Media Lab. It is available for free at https://scratch.mit.edu